SUCCESSFUL
TIME MANAGEMENT

SUCCESSFUL

TIME MANAGEMENT

FRANK ATKINSON

crimson

This edition first published in Great Britain 2009 by
Crimson Publishing, a division of Crimson Business Ltd
Westminster House
Kew Road
Richmond
Surrey
TW9 2ND

A catalogue record for this book is available from the British
Library.

ISBN 978 1 85458 526 4

Printed and bound by LegoPrint SpA, Trento

CONTENTS

INTRODUCTION

How often do we hear people say:

- 'I never have enough time!'
- 'I never have time to go to the gym. By the time I get home and eat dinner all I can do is crash out in front of the TV.'
- 'I never have enough time to myself, what with having the family to look after'.
- 'I never have enough time to spend with my team. We are always too busy.'
- 'I never have enough time to read a book. There are so many other priorities.'
- 'I never have enough time to cook, so I buy ready meals.'
- 'I never have enough time to train my staff. Other things always get in the way.'

All these regrets and grievances can be solved by successful time management.

This book is about time management. The purpose of this book is to give you the skills and techniques you need to manage your time more effectively. The main benefit from managing time effectively is not that you create time. That isn't possible. The main benefit is that it gives you more choice.

If you want to spend your leisure time watching TV or going online that is your choice. If you want to spend your time in the pub, with your friends, that is also your choice. The problem is that we sometimes look back and wish:

- 'I wish I'd spent more time with the kids.'
- 'I wish I'd learned Spanish at a night class.'
- 'I wish I had been a better manager.'
- 'I wish we'd spent more time as a family eating together.'
- 'I wish I'd spent more time looking after my relationships.'

What successful time management can do, as well as giving you the time to do the little things like go to the pub or read a book, is help you to make a definite plan, whether it is for your life or work, allowing you to achieve all those goals you seem to be always putting off.

By looking at your priorities and managing your time accordingly you will find that you are now able to achieve all the little things as well as the 'if only' dreams you felt you didn't have time for. This book will help you to manage your time, both in your life and your work in a way which will meet your priorities.

One of the objectives of this book is to try and persuade you, the reader, to reconsider how you are managing your life and to make changes that will make you more successful, happier and increase your sense of personal achievement.

PART 1

TIME MANAGEMENT BASICS

CHAPTER 1

Time management and your life

Managing time is about achieving balance. Most of us have to work and earn a living. This means getting the most from the working day, feeling that we have achieved something and getting the recognition we deserve. However, it is also about finding time to enjoy ourselves and achieve personal goals. This chapter will look at how successful time management can help in all areas of your life, be it work, family or some 'you time'. In this chapter we will define what we mean by time management and how it relates to you and how you manage your life. We will discuss the benefits of managing your time more effectively, look at the payback from being better organised and the importance of managing three important parts of your life:

- Your work
- Your friends and family
- You

IDENTIFYING YOUR PRIORITIES

Let us begin with a question:

'If you could improve your time management and gain an extra hour every day what would you do with it?'

Read more? Learn a language? Spend more quality time with friends and family? Do more exercise? Write a novel? Spend more time in bed? The issue here is that it is quite easy to find an extra hour a day. Set your alarm clock to go off an hour earlier. That's one way. However, the reality is more complicated than this.

The problem is that most of us spend too little time doing the important things in life. We fill up our day with activity, but does it get us anywhere? It is good, occasionally, to stop and think about what we want to achieve in our lives. What is the important stuff that we never get around to?

Let's begin by thinking about time. We all work under the same system in that there are 24 hours in each day. Time is not flexible. You can't stretch it, save it, keep some back for later on or buy it on eBay. Once it's gone it's gone. What you need to do to find that extra hour is to start managing and organising your time more efficiently.

ACTION POINT

Think of things that are important to you that you would really like to achieve. Now write down three goals. Think of:

- A goal that you would like to achieve in your work life

- A goal you would like to achieve in your family or personal life

- A goal that relates purely to you

For example, your **work goal** could be to earn a promotion, your **family goal** could be to visit Disneyland and your **you goal** could be to learn Spanish.

Write these down and we will come back to them later.

By way of an example I will tell you that my **you goal**, when I first did this exercise, was to run a half marathon. This was back in the nineties when running was becoming a big thing. The run I wanted to complete was the Great North Run, held in Newcastle. The first ever Great North Run had been staged on the 28th June 1981 and was devised by former Olympic 10,000m bronze medallist and BBC Sport commentator Brendan Foster. Thousands of people enter the event each year and I really wanted to take part.

The problem was that for years it remained a vague objective that never happened. I want to show you how I turned that vague want into reality and went on to complete over 30 half marathons.

Allocating time to our priorities

We all have dreams about achieving things. The reality is that we spend a disproportionate amount of our time doing things that don't really matter.

If you think about it we only have a limited amount of time to spend each week. Let's look at some figures:

- One week is 7 days x 24 hours = 168 hours.

- Assuming that we work a 40 hour week and travelling to and from work takes an hour a day = 45 hours.

- Assuming we sleep 9 hours a night = 63 hours.

- This leaves us with 60 hours a week for ourselves.

If we deduct the time we spend getting washed, dressed, eating, shopping, watching TV, time online and reading newspapers, this 60 hours is greatly reduced. Now, here's the real problem. It has been estimated the average European spends 14 hours a week online, 11 hours watching TV and 4.4 hours reading newspapers and magazines. This adds up to a whopping 29.4 hours a week[1].

That leaves us with only 30.6 hours to achieve all those goals and ambitions we dream of.

What does all this mean? It means we tend to fill up our life with activity without really thinking about whether our time is well spent. This is where good time management can make all the difference.

EVENTS BEYOND OUR CONTROL

A lot has been written about managing time. Time management books tend to focus on the importance of being well organised,

---

1 This is based on research carried out by the Forrester Research Group.

writing lists and having objectives. The problem is that you can only manage your time to a certain extent. Events interrupt our lives that make it impossible to fully control our time.

Random events completely beyond our control and devastate and change lives. When the Titanic sank there were a total of 2,223 people on board and out of those people, 1,517 died. This left only 706 survivors. Bernard Madoff, a prominent Wall Street trader, was arrested and accused of running a £33bn pyramid scheme that fooled some of the most prominent fund managers in the world. He got a prison sentence of 150 years. Not only has his life utterly changed but his actions have also changed the lives of the thousands of people who he swindled out of their life savings. People's lives changed and were ruined by events that they couldn't control. Fate plays a part in what happens to us in our lives. Or as the British comedian Ken Dodd once said 'If you want to see if God has a sense of humour tell him your future plans.' Our time can be interrupted by natural disasters or the actions of others. For most of us though we lose time due to simple everyday interruptions and events.

So, what can we do to manage our time? Firstly, we need to accept the fact that outside influences can get in the way of our plans. However, we also need to be aware that without a plan, our lives can drift and we can lose focus. We need to find a happy medium.

THE BENEFITS OF MANAGING YOUR TIME MORE EFFECTIVELY

At work

Frederick Herzberg was a clinical psychologist regarded as one of the great original thinkers in management and motivational theory. He found that certain factors made people satisfied, or dissatisfied, at work. He said that certain things motivated people, namely:

- Achievement

- Recognition

- The work itself

- Responsibility

- Promotion

He also found there were other issues that in themselves weren't motivators, but if they weren't satisfactory, they would de-motivate people. These were referred to as 'hygiene factors' and included things like:

- Salary

- Personal life

- Company policy

- Status

- Security

- Your relationship with other workers

- Your relationship with your supervisor

- Work conditions

Whether you are a manager, or a worker, what this said was that achievement and recognition are the things that motivate people most. If you are a manager, effective time management can ensure you have time to motivate your staff. This is good for you and for them. Similarly, if you are a worker, effective time management will give you a sense of achievement and get you the recognition you deserve.

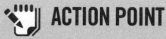

ACTION POINT

Think about what motivates you. Look at the list below and rank them in order of importance. This will help you to identify your priorities and help you to begin to manage your time to meet these priorities.

- Achievement
- Recognition
- The work itself
- Responsibility
- Promotion

Later on we will look at the importance of managing your manager (see p.53) and how to lead your team effectively (p.94).

Outside of work

Outside of work, effective time management has a number of benefits:

- It helps us to achieve more

- It makes us more motivated

- It helps us to recognise the important things in life

- It gives us focus

- It gives us a plan

- It helps us to motivate ourselves

GETTING STARTED

Motivation

Self-motivation is an interesting phenomenon. When I was training to run my half marathon I would sometimes come home from work and crash in front of the TV and try to get motivated

11

to get changed and start running. Often it didn't happen until a friend of mine told me 'don't wait for motivation. Motivation comes after action, not before it.' In other words I had to get out and do the exercise before I felt motivated. This is a really important point for time managers. We have to act. Begin the project and do it now.

Do it now

Don't spend your whole life writing lists. Begin work on projects, even if you can't complete them in one go. If an item appears more than three times on successive To Do lists consider dropping it, or begin working on it.

Q EXAMPLE

I recently moved house and work from home quite a bit. There is always work stuff to do, coffee to make, newspapers to read etc. What I have done is to set aside two hours a day to work on the house (more at weekends). Some of the jobs are short tasks that in themselves are not massively important, but here is the point, those two hour time slots really add up and things get done. As things get done our feeling of achievement and motivation increases.

Kerry Gleeson wrote the best-selling book *The Personal Efficiency Program* (John Wiley and Sons, 2009), which has two chapters, one called 'do it now' and the other called 'organise it now'. His main premise is that many jobs can be completed straight away in less time than it takes to organise, prioritise and update your To Do list. Like all time management tips I find it works in some situations and you need to work out how it applies to you and what you need to do differently.

It is often more productive to spend some time at the beginning of the working day getting rid of the small urgent tasks so that you are clear to tackle the more important stuff with a reduced, or empty To Do list.

TOP TIPS

How to get started:

- Begin by making your decision, 'I am going to manage my time'.
- Don't just focus on work. Think about managing your social time and think about you.
- Set yourself goals.
- Most people who save time go on to waste it. Think about what you really want to achieve.
- Don't try to manage every minute of every day. It won't work.

THE PAYBACK FROM BEING BETTER ORGANISED

The two main paybacks from being better organised are:

1. Increased motivation

2. Reduced stress

We have already discussed motivation. This comes from getting a sense of achievement when you accomplish your goals and move forward. Everyone is different and we are motivated by different things.

The other main payback is to reduce stress in our lives. We have all seen people under stress. They are in situations where they feel there are too many demands to cope with, or events are getting out of control. This can lead to health problems, loss of sleep and a feeling of being out of control.

Stress is actually the body's way of rising to a challenge and preparing to meet a tough situation with focus, strength, stamina, and heightened alertness. Events that provoke stress are called 'stressors', and they cover a whole range of situations. At work this could be making an important presentation, or having to meet a demanding target. There may also be people issues in the office that are causing stress.

When we feel stressed our body reacts by activating the nervous system and releasing certain hormones. These hormones have the effect of increasing our heart rate, breathing rate, blood pressure, and metabolism. During this process our blood vessels open up to let more blood flow to our muscles. Our body is preparing us for fight or flight. Our pupils dilate to improve our vision and sweat is produced to cool the body. All of these physical changes prepare us to react quickly and effectively to handle stressful situations.

This is the stress response and it helps us to perform more efficiently, however, it is not designed for the long term. When the body defences overreact, or don't turn off, this is when we get problems. Being better organised and having the right balance between life and work can reduce stress and make us feel calmer and better able to cope.

MANAGING YOUR TIME – THE BALANCE OF WORK, FAMILY AND FRIENDS, AND 'YOU'

Much of the writing on time management is focused on work issues. It puts forward ideas on managing your work time, managing your filing system, managing your desk and managing events; getting more of the important things done in the time available.

My view on time management is more holistic. There are three aspects to having a fulfilled life and it relates to the three key areas above; work, family and friends, and you.

The 'you' and 'family and friends' part of this is very important, although it may seem like we always give priority to work. Many people who raise families find their social time based around raising their kids. However, at some point the kids leave and what is left? Many couples find this hard to cope with and so it is better to invest some time in looking after you and your partner now rather than later. The current divorce rate in the UK is about 12%. This figure is down a bit on previous years, but one of the reasons for this fall has been the financial cost of divorce, so what this is saying is that many people in traditional relationships have problems. People don't invest enough time in managing their relationships and having time for themselves.

By following the tips and tools in this book you will be able to reconsider how you are managing your life and to make changes that will help you be more fulfilled at work and at home and put some time aside for yourself and your family and friends.

QUICK RECAP

- *Think about what you will do with the extra time you save.*

- *Time management can help you become better organised, however, outside influences can get in the way of your plans.*

- *Begin by setting yourself goals.*

- *Make sure that your goals relate to work, family and friends, and you.*

- *Think about the amount of time you spend online, watching TV and reading the papers. Are there other things you would rather be doing?*

- *Recognise that two of the main motivators are achievement and recognition. This applies to you and the people around you.*

- *Motivation comes after action, not before.*

- *Think about the concept of 'do it now' to achieve more and clear time for the more important stuff.*

- *Better time management will help reduce stress.*

CHAPTER 2

Goals

Most successful time managers have one thing in common: they have a very clear idea of where they want to go and how they are going to get there. In this chapter we will explore how important it is to have very clear goals in both your work and personal life. We will also see how it is important to turn your goals into a plan of action and to make that plan of action flexible so it can change as circumstances change.

THE IMPORTANCE OF SETTING GOALS

When I run my training courses I usually run a session at the beginning of each course on goal setting. I will ask the delegates to write down why they are attending the training course and what they want to achieve. In response one person recently said: 'I was sent and I don't know'. In a way this was quite sad. As trainers we get people like this all the time who are negative about training and make it very obvious that they would rather be somewhere else. It is a pity that some people have such a negative attitude towards learning. Learning is a lifelong experience and one of our life goals should be to take advantage of every learning opportunity that presents itself. This example goes to show that by not setting goals we can waste opportunities to manage our time effectively.

So, why are goals important both in life and in business? As the saying goes: 'if you don't know where you are going, how are you going to know when you've got there?'

🔍 EXAMPLE

In the book What They Don't Teach You in the Harvard Business School, *Mark McCormack tells of a study conducted on students in the 1979 Harvard MBA program.*

In that year, the students were asked, 'have you set clear, written goals for your future and made plans to accomplish them?' Only 3% of the graduates had written goals and plans; 13% had goals, but they were not in writing; and 84% had no specific goals at all.

Ten years later, the members of the class were interviewed again, and the findings, while somewhat predictable, were nonetheless astonishing. The 13% of the class who had goals were earning, on average, twice as much as the 84% who had no goals at all.

And what about the 3% who had clear, written goals? They were earning, on average, 10 times as much as the other 97% put together.

HOW DO YOU START?

To begin goal setting you need to think about your life and what you want to achieve. Different things are important to different people. Here are some areas you might want to think about:

- Career goals
- Family goals
- Health goals
- Learning goals
- Social goals
- Financial goals

Some of this goal setting will be personal to you while some will involve other people.

Goals should be **SMART**:

- Specific
- Measurable
- Achievable
- Relevant
- Time bound

Q EXAMPLE

Let's say your goal is something like 'I want to get fit'. Ask yourself if it is SMART:

*Is it **specific**?: No.*

How fit do you want to get and how will you know when you've achieved your goal? To do this you are going to need to set some performance measures.

*Is it **measurable**?: Not at the moment, but it could be. Maybe you could set a more detailed target. It could be as part of this process you decide to join the local running club as you are aware that they train three evenings a week and run about three miles each time they meet. This is easier to measure.*

*Is it **achievable**? Yes.*

*Is it **relevant**? Yes.*

*Is it **time bound**? No, so you need to set some timescales on this particular goal.*

At the moment the goal doesn't fit the SMART criteria. It is not specific and it is not measurable.

A better goal might be to say: 'I will join the local running club this week, train three nights a week, and in six months time I will give myself the target to run six miles in under 60 minutes.'

The SMART criteria are an important part of goal setting. Many people don't have goals at all. That is their choice but as you have bought this book it is fair to assume that you want to make changes to the way you run your life so you will be open to devising goals.

Some people have vague goals that often begin with the words 'One day...':

- 'One day, when the kids have gone we will travel more.'

- 'One day I am going to write a novel.'

- 'One day I am going to look at the possibility of doing a degree.'

But these goals will probably never be achieved.

What the SMART criteria do is to focus our mind on the **what** and the **when**. However, this is only the start of the goal setting process. Once you have defined your goal write it down and tell other people about it. Written goals are more likely to be achieved, as are goals that we share with others. Now you need to write your plan, start putting it into practice and amend the plan as necessary.

HOW LONG TERM SHOULD MY GOALS BE?

It is important to have long, medium and short-term goals. The long-term goals could be 10, or 20 years ahead depending on the particular goal. This could be something like 'I want to be financially secure by the time I am 55'. If this event is 20 years away you need to start thinking about your medium-term goals and then your short term goals. This way you have an aim in sight, but also have plans in place to get you there.

The process of goal setting is about having clear objectives, having a plan to achieve those objectives and acting on the plan, amending it as you go along. People without goals tend to achieve less than those who do have them. However, even if you have goals, you need a plan of action, and because circumstances change, your plan needs to be acted upon and amended as necessary.

CAREER GOALS

Setting goals for your career is very important. To plan your career you need to be thinking about a number of issues then putting your plan into place.

SWOT analysis

First of all, start by doing a SWOT analysis on yourself to find out the kind of career that will suit you best or to work out the parts of your job you enjoy the most. A SWOT analysis is a marketing tool that looks at:

- Strengths

- Weaknesses

- Opportunities

- Threats

Strengths: What are you good at and what do you enjoy doing? If you are the outdoor type would you suit an office job? If you are a caring person would you suit life on the trading floor of a merchant bank? Don't just take your own word for it. Ask someone you trust to give you some feedback. It is really important in your career that you enjoy what you do and are suited for your chosen profession.

Weaknesses: What are you not so good at? Are your weaknesses something you can change? Are they allowable weaknesses?

Opportunities: What opportunities are out there that could help you build your desired career? Do you know people who could help you? Are there organisations that have resources you could tap into? A useful piece of advice to consider is that to be successful, you should find somebody who is already successful in your chosen field and mirror the things they do.

Threats: What is stopping you from achieving your goal? Are there certain industries that don't have a long-term future? Are there outside influences that would prevent you from being successful? Might a lack of financial resources be a problem for getting into certain professions?

There are other issues to be aware of when looking at your career goals, some of which may answer some of the weaknesses or opportunities identified by your SWOT analysis.

Education and training

Some professions require education to degree level then further professional qualifications. But the education we get at school doesn't always equip us to deal with life at work. What we also find is that once we have been given a job, it is our performance, rather than formal qualifications that moves us up the career ladder. Look into any training courses you can do that will help improve your performance.

Promote yourself

It used to be that a well written CV was all that you needed. Now, with the growth of the internet, there are other ways to promote yourself. You can have your own website, and promote yourself on one or all of the social and business networking sites that we see all over the internet. Blogs are also a good way of getting you known and there are many opportunities to post articles on the internet to enhance your reputation.

Become an expert

It doesn't matter what career you choose, if you are seen as being an expert, people will find you.

Network

It is a very powerful career building tool to have a network of friends, business colleagues and contacts who can help you manage your career.

FAMILY GOALS

Many families like to sit down and plan their goals together. Individual needs change as the family grows older and when the hormones start to kick in. The goal setting process is very similar to that for your career goals, although possibly a bit more informal.

In my family we used to sit down at the beginning of each year and write a list of things we wanted to do as a family. We used to stick this list on the inside of one of the kitchen cupboard doors and cross off each item as it was achieved. Every time we opened the cupboard we got a reminder of the goal situation and it was a spur to get things done.

TOP TIPS

Make sure your family goals involve everyone and you all have a role to play in achieving them.

HEALTH GOALS

A lot of our goals can be interlinked and some can be achieved more quickly than others. Personally, most of my health goals have been based around losing weight and getting fit, although friends have looked at other health issues such as having a healthier diet and doing more exercise.

The key here is for your goals to be ambitious but achievable and realistic. For example if you set the goal of swimming a mile every day for the rest of your life, it will not happen. It is far better to set a more realistic goal that is achievable and then exceed your expectations rather than to be too ambitious and fail.

Q EXAMPLE

A friend of mine decided to try the Atkins diet, but because he liked to eat out he decided to use the Atkins method Monday to Friday only (which means the diet is not achievable because he wasn't following its strict guidelines). He also didn't set himself a target of weight loss, so it wasn't measurable. Needless to say he didn't lose any weight and soon went back to his old ways.

LEARNING GOALS

Our learning goals will probably change as we get older. What have you always wanted to learn? It could be a skill like learning to cook, or speaking another language, or it could be more knowledge based around learning about history, your local area, or travelling to foreign parts and learning about other cultures.

SOCIAL GOALS

Our social goals are based around time spent away from work and deal with relationships and having a positive social life. In 2006 13% of people living in the UK lived alone. A social goal could involve you joining a club or reconnecting with old friends. The social and family network is changing with more and more people managing their social life online. See if you can find any lost friends and make a connection through one of the many social networks available now.

Goal setting is about achieving balance. If this book makes you question your goals, or lack of them then it is time to move to the next stage, which is to write down your plan.

FINANCIAL GOALS

With financial goals there is always the dilemma of how much you are prepared to give up today in order to look after tomorrow. Increasingly in the UK people have seen their future security threatened by mistakes made by government and our financial institutions.

As people live longer strains on social welfare mean that future generations will have to take more responsibility for their own welfare as they get older, meaning clear financial goals are more important than ever. Although it can be difficult to consider when your worries are focused on the present, look into setting up a pension plan or a savings account. The future will come around quicker than you think!

Acting on your goals

It is important to begin with your overall long-term goal and then break it down into a series of smaller goals. Take each smaller goal in turn and brainstorm all the possible actions you will need to take to achieve each goal.

These actions can then be put into order and acted upon.

✍ ACTION POINT

Getting started in setting goals:

1. Begin by writing a list of your overall goals: be it career, health, family etc.

2. Break the list down into smaller sub-goals, making sure they are achievable and measurable.

3. Brainstorm, in no particular order, all the things that will need to happen for the goal to be achieved.

4. Put these into a logical order, or sequence.

5. Put together your plan of action, along with measurable timelines.

6. Begin acting on your plan. Schedule time into your diary to make sure things happen.

7. Amend the plan as circumstances change (which they will).

8. Keep others informed of your progress.

9. Reward yourself as the plan starts to become a reality.

On achieving your goals

• Try to visualise the outcome you are looking to achieve. How will it make you feel?

• Think about how you will feel if nothing changes.

• Begin working on your goals now.

• Don't let other people's negative thinking put you off.

• Think positive.

• Reward yourself when you achieve your goals.

• Try to avoid situations that trigger the situation or action you are trying to change.

ACHIEVING YOUR WORK-LIFE BALANCE

This is a phrase we hear a lot and it is considered a good thing to balance out the demands of work and the need to have an active social life, but what does it actually mean?

What it doesn't mean is that you plan rigidly to spend equal amounts of time working, playing and sleeping. This is unrealistic. What it does mean is that there will be times when you have to focus more on work issues, for example if the company you work for is having problems, or they have just won a big order that needs shipping urgently you may need to spend more time at work. On the other hand if your kids are sick you may need to negotiate some extra time off work, or rearrange how you organise your workload, shifting the balance of your time towards family life.

However, you may be under pressure to work longer hours because of the culture of the organisation you work for, meaning you will have to find other ways to balance your time rather than simply asking. There is a moderately new phenomenon which has been labelled 'presenteeism'. It is the opposite of 'absenteeism' and is seen a lot in IT and financial organisations, where downsizing has meant that there are fewer people to do the work and brownie points can be earned for working late and starting work early. This is often seen as a measure of the individual's commitment to the business, but can result in increased stress and medical problems. The key question is how to balance these competing priorities; and this is something that both goal setting and effective time management will help you do.

QUICK RECAP

- *Successful time managers have clearly defined goals.*

- *Goals can cover all aspects of our work and non-work lives.*

- *Goals need to be SMART (Specific, Measurable, Achievable, Relevant, Time bound).*

- *Goals should be a mix of long, medium and short-term.*

- *Goal setting begins with an overall objective which is then broken down into a series of smaller goals.*

- *This leads to an action plan, which must be put into practice.*

- *The plan should be flexible and amended over time as things change.*

- *Your work-life balance is important and is about achieving a balance between achievement and enjoyment.*

CHAPTER 3

Getting started

In this chapter we will show you how to get started and begin changing the way you do things. You'll need to think about what you want to change and why. What are the paybacks you are looking to achieve and how do you motivate yourself to get started?

We'll also reveal the greatest source of your time management problems. This might just surprise you. Finally, we need to think about what you can and can't control. Time management can help to deal with stress, but it can't stop things happening that are outside our control.

WHAT PREVENTS US FROM CHANGING THINGS?

So what is it that prevents us from changing? We all know that we should change various aspects of our lives, but often we never get around to making the first move. All change involves an element of risk. There are four main reasons why we don't change things:

1. Fear of failure

2. Fear of success

3. The enormity of the task

4. Other people

Fear of failure

We worry that we are not going to succeed and that prevents us from trying in the first place. This can be based on previous negative experiences.

Fear of success

Sometimes it is easier to leave things as they are. We prefer to stay in our comfort zone.

The enormity of the task

Sometimes the enormity of a task makes us think it is best left undone. We look at all the time and effort needed to complete the task and give up. The key is to break big tasks down into smaller tasks and begin working on them. Keep in mind: 'How do you eat an elephant? One mouthful at a time!'

Other people

Other people can influence our self-esteem and confidence. It is very important to develop a positive self-image so that you have the confidence to change things. The view we have of ourselves is often developed in childhood by those people who most influence our behaviour and our lives.

SO HOW DO WE GET STARTED?

Let's start by looking at you. You may have a job or a career, you may have a family and friends, or you may just have friends. If you look at everyone's life and circumstances they are all different, so I am not assuming that everyone reading this book has a wife/ husband, kids, a job, a mortgage and plays golf. What this chapter will do is give some broad principles that anyone can adapt to suit their lifestyle.

A lot of the time when I work with companies as a consultant, they want to make things change. The process I use is to find the answers to four questions:

1. Where are you now?

2. Where would you like to get to?

3. How are you going to get there?

4. What's in it for you if it works?

🔍 EXAMPLE

Let's take a simple example of a goal 'I want to learn to speak Spanish' and apply these four questions:

1. Where are you now?

'I currently only have a few words and phrases and have to rely on others speaking English when I am in Spain.'

This answer is a clear statement of where you are at the moment before you go on to devise your action plan of how you are going to achieve your goal.

2. Where would I like to get to?

'I want to learn to speak Spanish and achieve a B grade GCSE pass within 18 months.'

As we saw in chapter 2 we need to make goals SMART. This answer is specific, measurable, achievable, relevant and time bound.

3. How am I going to get there?

The next step is to begin putting together your action plan and putting it into practice as we described previously. This means writing down all the things that you have to do to achieve your goal. This could include things like:

- *Find someone to study with*

- *Assess the local facilities for adult learning*

- *Check out what other resources are available*

- *Find out how to apply for a course*

- *Assess different study methods; online, local college, distance learning, private tutor*

- *Find out how you apply to take a GCSE*

- *Check out the timescales involved. How long will it take?*

- *Find out how much it will cost?*

- *What time commitment is required?*

Then begin to prepare your action plan by putting the above points into a logical order and putting time deadlines to each item.

4. What's in it for me if it works?
Now you need to ask yourself if achieving this goal will really be worth all the time and effort. Will learning Spanish have a positive impact in your life?

Now ask yourself three questions:

1. Why do you want to learn Spanish?

2. What paybacks will you receive when you have achieved your goal?

3. What is stopping you from changing?

In this example the answers are:

1. *I like to go to Spain on holiday and I would like to be able to talk to Spanish people in their own language when I am there.*

2. *The main payback is that I will feel more confident and it will give me a buzz to see their reaction.*

3. *I keep meaning to start but either don't have the time, or don't know the best way to go about it.*

 ACTION POINT

Identify one thing that you've been putting off doing.
Ask yourself:

1. Where are you now?

2. Where would you like to get to?

3. How are you going to get there?

4. What's in it for you if it works?

Remember to look at your motivations and how you will feel when you achieve your goal.

It is better if you do this exercise with a partner as it can be a really interesting and fun experience.

GETTING MOTIVATED

Self-motivation is always a problem when setting and achieving goals. How is it that some people seem to be always highly motivated and others the exact opposite?

There are a number of theories that we can look at but my favourite is very simple. I do a lot of driving with my job and buy CDs and cassettes to listen to on my travels. A few years ago I bought a cassette on motivation by someone called Atkinson (no relation, although when I talk about Atkinson's theory of motivation it sounds pretty impressive!)

The theory comes in two parts:

Part one comes in the form of an equation:
Motivation = Desire X Expectation of success.

Part two says that action comes first and motivation follows.

Look at the first part, with regards to being motivated to learn Spanish. If you don't really want to do it and have no real desire to put in the effort it is unlikely you will even start. Or else you may order the five CD set on learning Spanish and never actually begin listening to it.

If your expectation of success is low and you think you will probably fail it is unlikely you will have sufficient motivation to achieve your goal and learn to speak Spanish.

In other words before you begin your action plan ask yourself two questions:

1. Do I really want to do this?

2. Do I think I will succeed?

The second part of the theory says that motivation follows action. In other words it is no good waiting for motivation to kick in and then act. Get started on your plan and the motivation will follow.

Make sure your goal is important to you and that you feel you have a good chance of achieving it. Try and work out why you want to achieve your goal and what the payoffs might be. Finally, try to work out what is stopping you from taking some form of action right now.

THE BIGGEST SOURCE OF YOUR TIME MANAGEMENT PROBLEMS

When I run my time management courses I often ask the question 'what is the biggest source of your time management problems?' We do it as a brainstorming exercise and typical answers are:

• Interruptions

• Phone calls

• Emails

• Meetings

• Computer down time

• Administration

• Paperwork

• My boss

• People who work for me

• Unplanned events

When I run this point, having put all these points on the flip chart I challenge the group by saying they have failed to identify their major source of time management problems.

Your major source of time management problems is **YOU**.

Yes, all the items listed are important and can get in the way of effective time management, but the way you behave and the way you organise your time affects you and the people around you.

Personality types

There are different personality types who organise their time in different ways and therefore have different ways of disrupting their own time and that of those around them:

1. You are the sort of person who finds it hard to say no and are not very assertive. You work in an open plan office and you have a colleague who works nearby who continually comes over to you to gossip and talk about their social life. Being the sort of person you are you let them get away with wasting your time and you are late in finishing a report for your manager.

2. You are the sort of person who is first in the office and last to leave. You like to keep yourself busy and often take on work for other people because you like to be on the go all the time. However, at your latest appraisal your manager has said that while you are a valued hard working member of the team you have failed to achieve some of your key objectives because you say you were too busy.

3. You are a perfectionist. You can't bear shoddy work so you insist on checking out all correspondence that leaves your department. You have a report to write each month for your board of directors which takes a few days of your time to get right. You have been told that the board members regularly fail to read the report and that one of the directors produces his own one page summary to save time.

4. You are a very strong person. You don't suffer fools gladly and you don't believe in socialising with members of your team. You are not a particularly good delegator because you don't trust them to do as good a job as you. You expect high standards of the team and expect them to work late when you tell them to even though they may have other plans.

5. You like to work under pressure. In fact, if you have weeks to do a job, or project you will often leave it until the last minute, because it gives you more of a buzz. You are regularly late for meetings and are often in trouble with your manager for just missing deadlines.

Do you recognise yourself in any of these scenarios?

In the book by or Eric Berne, *Games People Play: The Psychology of Human Relationships*, he describes how our behaviour is influenced by our childhood experiences and identifies five personal drivers, or working styles.

The five drivers are:

- Please people
- Try hard
- Be perfect
- Be strong
- Hurry up

If you have a **Please people driver** you like people to be happy and you are therefore a good team player. You like to help others and like to be liked. However, all the drivers I am going to describe have a positive and a negative side. If your Please people driver is too strong you can let others take advantage of your good nature. You don't like to upset people and find it very hard to say no. This can influence your time management which is often controlled by others if you are not careful.

If you have a **Try hard driver** you love new projects and can work under pressure. You are capable of handling a big workload and like the challenge that hard work brings. However, the down side is that you take on too much and fail to complete certain tasks.

Being effective is not just about working hard, it is also about working smart and prioritising tasks rather than trying to do everything.

If you have a **Be perfect driver** you are excellent at doing accurate and detailed work to a high degree of quality. You spend a lot of time getting things right. The danger is that sometimes a Be perfect approach isn't appropriate. Deadlines have to be met and Be perfect people can put themselves under a lot of unnecessary pressure and often miss deadlines.

The **Be strong driver** is great for crisis managers who need to keep a steady nerve under pressure. This person leads from the front and doesn't show much emotion, but gets on with the task in hand. The downside of Be strong is that you can be difficult to work with. Be strong managers get good results, but often at the expense of other team members and team spirit.

If you have a **Hurry up driver** you can work to tight deadlines and work quickly to achieve your goals. You are quite happy to do things at the last moment and suit an environment that is fast moving and demanding. You always seem to do things at the last moment. The reality is that Hurry up people only get a buzz if there is time pressure to do a job and will often leave jobs to the last minute because it gives them a buzz.

Usually two of these drivers most strongly influence the way we behave. Some combinations are compatible, such as Hurry up and Try hard, while others can conflict. Imagine having a Be perfect and Hurry up as your main drivers.

Once you recognise what drives your behaviour, you can start to identify how this affects your style of working and your time management.

TOP TIPS

 ACTION POINT

Talk to your partner or a friend about your working and time management styles. Try to identify each others' drivers and how they affect the way you manage your time.

WHAT CAN WE DO WITH THIS KNOWLEDGE?

Firstly, try to decide which of the drivers best describe your behaviour. Can you think of examples where your drivers have caused you time management problems in the past? For example:

• Failing to meet deadlines

• Taking on too high a workload

• Being given jobs to do that are not your responsibility

• Feeling under pressure

Here are some ideas for changing the way you work, depending on your personal drivers.

Please people person

If you are a Please people person stop trying to keep everybody happy. Learn to say no. This means taking a few risks as it is always easier just to keep doing the same old things. However, as they say: 'If you always do what you always did, you'll always get what you always got'.

How to say no:

- Stop feeling guilty. You have a right to say no.

- Explain why you can't do what they want you to do. Be objective and factual.

- Look for an alternative: 'I can't do this now, but why don't we look at our priorities?'

- Make eye contact during the conversation. It makes you look more confident.

Try hard person

If you are a Try hard sort of person think about working smarter. Speak with your manager and agree priorities and realistic time scales. Identify the important tasks and, occasionally, leave some tasks uncompleted.

Be perfect person

For the Be perfects, try not to waste time making unimportant tasks perfect. Prioritise your work and use your Be perfect skills on the important stuff.

Be strong person

If you have a Be strong driver think about the effect this has on others. Play to your strengths, but give praise to others when they do a good job and try to understand their time management needs. Loosen up. Talk to others if you have a problem.

Hurry up person

If you recognise that you are a Hurry up person set time deadlines to ensure you are not leaving things until the last minute. Negotiate more time to do certain tasks if you need to and understand how your Hurry up approach can have a negative influence on others.

If you want to change the way you behave try and find a low risk situation to practise your new behaviour.

TOP TIPS

Q EXAMPLE

I used to have a secretary who was a fantastic worker. She was a Try hard and Be perfect person. The standard of her work was excellent and always of top quality. The problem was my Hurry up driver. I would give her work to do at the last minute and she used to get very upset and frustrated. One day she handed in her resignation, which shocked me as I didn't realise there was a problem.

We ended up by negotiating a better way of working which meant she had time to do her work well and she wasn't getting last minute surprises dumped on her desk. It's important to consider how others work as well as your own style of working to find the best time management strategies for everyone.

QUICK RECAP

- *Identify reasons why you don't change things; fear of failure, fear of success, the size of the task and the influence of others.*

- *Go through the four key questions to begin the process of change:*
  - *Where am I now?*
  - *Where would I like to get to?*
  - *How am I going to get there?*
  - *What's in it for me if it works?*

- *Motivation is about our desire and our expectations of success.*

- *Motivation comes after action, not before.*

- *Your biggest source of time management problems is you!*

- *Try to identify which of the five drivers relate to you:*
  - *Please people*
  - *Try hard*
  - *Be perfect*
  - *Be strong*
  - *Hurry up*

- *Start working on your drivers. Accentuate the positives, eliminate the negatives.*

CHAPTER 4

Setting priorities

One of the problems with managing time is knowing how to plan each day and, as the day progresses, deciding what to do next. What you have to choose is which activity should take priority and get done now. In this chapter we will explore how to set priorities, how to deal with competing priorities and the importance of managing your manager.

IDENTIFYING PRIORITIES

In the medium to long term there may be projects that require a lot of time and effort, while in the short term we often have a never ending list of small tasks which can be done quickly but use up precious time. What is the best way to fit the projects which require more time and effort into a busy schedule with all the conflicting pressures on your time?

We all face choices and decisions that we have to make about managing our time, many times each day. Personally, I find that while it is easy to fill my time with activity and be busy, there are times when I look back and wonder if all that effort has actually achieved anything. Also, I am sure, like me, there are things you always wished you had done but never got round to them.

If you have a busy job or social life there are choices that you need to make when you are planning your time. It would be nice to be able to plan everything logically and work to a pre-prepared schedule, but life has a habit of getting in the way. Everyone has 24 hours in each day. During that time we have to work, sleep, spend time with loved ones and spend a bit of time with ourselves. Why is it that some people seem to be so well organised and achieve so much, while others never seem to get what they want done? It's all about identifying your priorities and then managing your time to suit them.

PRIORITIES AND YOUR JOB PURPOSE

The reason you need to be clear about your job purpose is to ensure that when you are setting priorities and deciding what to do next, that you can answer the question 'Is this next task I am about to start moving me nearer to achieving my job purpose, or not?' If it is, we define the task as being important. This is a specific definition for the purpose of managing your time. A job may need to be done and you may have to do it, but if it doesn't move you nearer to achieving your job purpose it is considered not important.

Q EXAMPLE

Recently, I was working with Jan, who works in customer services for a financial services company in London. She has a very busy job answering customer queries and helping solve problems. At one point she said in a very frustrated voice 'I wish the phone would stop ringing so I could get on with my work'.

The problem was that her frustration was very obvious in her tone of voice and was affecting the way she was responding to her customers. Customers with problems don't want to talk to someone who is not concerned, or who seems to want to be doing something else.

I had to point out to her, very diplomatically, that her job was answering the phone and that because of the nature of her job we had to look at different ways of her managing her time so that her customers continued to receive the service they deserved, but that she could also feel she was achieving her objectives.

She needed, first of all to decide exactly what the purpose of her job was. This is the first step in learning how to set priorities and deal with conflicting priorities.

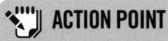 **ACTION POINT**

You need to figure out 'what is the purpose of my job?'
Write down in a single sentence what your job is and why it
exists. For example, if you are in sales your job purpose could be
something like 'To achieve my sales targets as agreed with my sales
manager, to retain existing clients and to grow my client base by
10% each year'.

Write down your job purpose. Keep it simple. Show it to your
manager and get their agreement that it is correct.

URGENT VS IMPORTANT

Another aspect of looking at priorities is to decide whether a
particular task has a deadline attached to it. If it has a timescale
it is classified as being **urgent** and should be considered a priority.

By combining important, not important, urgent and not urgent we
can get four categories of task, which can be combined into what
we call the **priority grid**[2].

	Important	Not Important
Urgent	Important and Urgent	Urgent but Not Important
Not Urgent	Important but Not Urgent	Not Important and Not Urgent

2 This is based on work done by Steven Covey in his book 7 *Habits of Highly
Effective People* published by Free Press.

ACTION POINT

If you had four tasks to choose between; one from each quadrant, what order would you do them in? Write down your order of preference.

Most people say what they would do first is to tackle the task that is *important and urgent*. An example could be to present your business plan to your board of directors at their meeting on Thursday at 3pm. These are things that **must** be done **now** or very soon and take precedence over everything else.

The preferred next choice of most people is the *important, not urgent* task. These are the jobs that we keep putting off that can make a real difference to our effectiveness at work. An example could be to appraise the performance of members of your team.

Most people say they would then tackle the *urgent but not important task*. An example here could be to fill in your expense forms. These may have a deadline, but the task, in itself, doesn't move you nearer to achieving your job purpose. The built-in time limits to these tasks ensure that these things do get done. The key is to do them as quickly as possible with the minimum quality required.

The final category that people say they would tackle is the *not important, not urgent task*. An example could be to make a coffee for yourself at work. There are many things that are neither important nor urgent. We often do them because they give us the feeling of activity, or being busy doing something.

This is not what happens in real life!

In reality, what happens is that people prioritise based on urgency rather than importance. What they actually do is different to what they say they would do.

The order most people prioritise tasks in real life is:

1. Important and Urgent
2. Urgent but Not Important
3. Not Urgent and Not Important
4. Important but Not Urgent

The real lesson here is that in reality, what gets left till last or doesn't get done at all are the important, not-urgent tasks. Most of the really important things in our lives are not urgent; they can be done now or later. In many cases they can be postponed forever, and in too many cases they are. Examples of these are long range planning, improving systems, self-improvement, writing an article, or improving relationships. This is the area that truly determines effectiveness.

Competing priorities

Where you have competing priorities, say for example you identify three important not urgent tasks, these in turn must be prioritised so you can begin working on the most important task first.

When we observe people at work, we see that most people set priorities according to urgency and this usually leads to three categories:

1. Must be done today
2. Should be done today
3. To be done sometime

Try setting priorities first in terms of importance by asking yourself:

- Does this activity contribute directly to the purpose of my job?

- Does it have a bearing on my short-term objectives?

- Will it help me achieve my personal goals?

Having determined the importance of the tasks you should prioritise them according to how well they answer these three questions.

TIME/BENEFIT RATIO

A final consideration when setting your priorities is the Time/ Benefit ratio. This is the idea that unimportant and perhaps non-urgent things are sometimes best done now, thereby leaving you free for more vital things. Sometimes you can't begin to work on important items until you have an uninterrupted block of time. So, for example you may have an important project, but the person you need to talk to is not available for an hour or so. Use these blocks of time to get rid of your not important, not urgent tasks because they tend to be easy to finish quickly. This also has the benefit of giving the illusion of achieving something as items on your To Do list are removed.

Have you heard of the Pareto principle? Vilfredo Pareto was an Italian philosopher who noted that 80% of the land in Italy was owned by 20% of the population. Management thinkers have taken the basic principle and applied it to a number of work activities. In sales terms, 80% of our business comes from 20% of our customer base. In production terms, 80% of product problems are caused by 20% of product defects and so on. Therefore 80% of our effective work is done in 20% of our time. Note the word *effective*.

What this tells us is that we can be more effective by changing the way we prioritise work through identifying exactly what makes up the less effective 80% of how we spend our time. No one can be 100% efficient and there are things that have to be done that don't directly contribute to our job purpose. By making small alterations in the way we prioritise our time we can achieve more.

TOP TIPS

Next time you make a list of things to do, remember, if there are 10 items on your list completing the two most important tasks will probably have the same impact as completing the other eight.

✏️ ACTION POINT

Analyse the following 10 statements. For each statement decide which they category they fall under:

1. Important and Urgent
2. Urgent but Not Important
3. Not Urgent and Not Important
4. Important but Not Urgent

Statement	Category
1. I must read the paper 2. I must attend the management training course next month 3. I must prepare some induction training for new staff members 4. I must update my CV by next week 5. I must go down and put some more money in the parking meter 6. I must learn how to be more assertive with my manager 7. I must train the sales team on objection handling at today's meeting 8. I must review the way we deal with customer complaints 9. I must learn how to use Outlook 10. I must get my hair cut	

Answers: although open to interpretation, most people say that statements 2 and 7 are important and urgent, 4 and 5 urgent but not important, 3,6 and 9 important not urgent and 1 and 10 not important and not urgent.

Learning how to prioritise your work according to its urgency and importance will help you to manage your time more successfully and work more effectively.

MANAGING YOUR MANAGER

Managing your manager is an important part of setting priorities at work. Most of us, unless we run our own business, have a manager to report to. One of the most common faults of managers is that they often set very unclear objectives for the people they manage. Some managers set objectives but keep changing them. If you are going to have a clear idea of your priorities, your manager needs to be involved. Also, if you have conflicting, or competing priorities there needs to be clarification so you know you are doing what is required of you.

I used to have a manager who was badly organised and did not set clear objectives. He would give me projects and then forget about them because he had taken up a new idea. This was very frustrating. I realised early on in our relationship I needed to meet with him on a regular basis and agree my objectives; we called them 30 day achievables. I would also give him regular written feedback on my progress. I shouldn't have had to do this but it made our working relationship more effective.

While it is right to tackle jobs in terms of their importance rather than their urgency, there are barriers to setting priorities that can frustrate your efforts to become a better time manager:

- You have unclear objectives

- You have conflicting objectives

- You have too big a workload

- You have insufficient resources (money/people/technology)

- You lack certain skills

- You work in a very reactive environment where things constantly change

This is where you need to have the confidence to manage your manager. In chapter 10 we will look at how to be more assertive. Being assertive means getting what you want and need without being aggressive. It is about having the confidence to meet with your manager and ask certain questions like:

- What do you want me to achieve in the next month, six months, and in the next year?

- What are my priorities?

- How are we going to measure my progress and how often?

- What standards of performance will you measure me by?

- How will we communicate with each other?

- What training will I need to do the job well?

- What resources will I be given?

- How often do we need to meet to discuss progress?

You need to understand, as does your manager, that there will probably not be enough time to do everything, so you must find the time to do the most important things.

TOP TIPS

Manage the communication between you and your manager. Agree how often you need to meet and set an agenda for each meeting. Despite the fact that you may work in the same office, it is still important to meet formally on a regular basis to discuss progress. The most common cry for help I hear when working with clients is members of staff saying 'I don't know how I am doing!'

QUICK RECAP

- *Make sure you manage your work and social time.*

- *Identify your priorities and order them accordingly.*

- *Begin by writing down your job purpose. This defines what your job is and where you should be concentrating your efforts.*

- *Categorise tasks in terms of their importance and urgency.*

- *Important and urgent tend to get done because they have a deadline.*

- *Not important and urgent tend to be done next because they also have a deadline.*

- *Not important and not urgent tasks tend to be done next because they tend to be easy to complete.*

- *Important but not urgent tasks tend to get left undone unless we give them a deadline.*

- *Important and urgent tasks include planning, reviewing, developing your skills, improving systems, self- development and improving relationships.*

- *The Pareto principle says 80% of our effective work is done in 20% of our time.*

- *Manage your manager. Seek guidance on your objectives and their expectations.*

CHAPTER 5

Putting a plan together

'Would you tell me which way I ought to go from here?' asked Alice.

'That depends a good deal on where you want to get to,' said the Cat.

'I don't much care where' replied Alice.

'Then it doesn't much matter which way you go' said the Cat.

Lewis Carroll, *Alice's Adventures in Wonderland*

This chapter will provide key information on how to produce a plan to manage your time and achieve your goals. We will introduce two types of plan and provide templates to help you produce your own plans, whether they are for business, or for your life outside work.

REASONS WE DON'T PLAN

I am sure you have probably heard the cliché 'failing to plan is planning to fail'. So what prevents us from planning the important things in life?

For one thing, planning is one of those important, but not urgent tasks described in chapter 4 (see p.48). We all agree it is a good thing, but most people never get round to it. Here are some reasons we don't plan:

- Planning is boring. It is easier to act than to think.

- We lack the motivation to plan.

- Planning can be quite a difficult process. Do we really know what we want?

- We expect planning to be perfect, but most plans are imperfect and we rarely achieve everything we plan for.

Although it is easy to accept these reasons and avoid planning there are several benefits of planning which make for successful time management.

BENEFITS AND ADVANTAGES OF PLANNING

The main benefit of planning, whether in business or in life, is that it helps us to focus our attention on where we are going and how we are going to get there. Many people are happy to take life as it comes and don't see the importance of planning, but if we are going to achieve more of the important not urgent things in life we need to plan.

Here are some of the advantages planning can give:

- A way forward. A goal, or set of goals to work towards.

- More focus on the really important things we want to achieve in life and at work.

- A clearly defined action plan broken down into the short, medium, and long-term objectives.

- Estimates of timescales involved in achieving those objectives.

- Ideas of the costs involved of achieving our objectives, both in terms of finance and time.

- A view of the obstacles we may face along the way.

- A clear view of our role and responsibilities in helping to make the plan a success.

- Better management of our time because we now have a target to aim at and an action plan in place.

SHORT, MEDIUM AND LONG-TERM GOALS

When coming up with a plan it is important to split it into short, medium and long-term goals so that we achieve all our urgent and important and important but not urgent tasks.

Why are our **short-term goals** important? Our short-term goals tell us what we should be doing this week, or this month, to achieve our short-term objectives. In business this is important as it can influence issues such as orders received, production targets met, accounts produced and cash flow maintenance that are required for the business to function on a day to day basis.

Why are our **medium-term goals** important? By looking at the medium-term we are released from the urgent day to day stuff and can begin to plan without having to worry about short-term issues. Medium-term goals are a stepping stone to the longer term stuff, with more time to think and plan.

Why are our **long-term goals** important? In business we need to have a vision of the future. Where are we going on the long journey ahead? Where do we see ourselves in 10, 15, or 20 years time?

PLANNING FOR BUSINESS

Creating a vision statement

One of the first steps to creating a plan of action is to create a vision statement, a way of clearly stating where you see yourself or your business in the future.

For any business to succeed, it must know what it is about. It must be able to clearly describe why it is there, and what it is there to achieve. Developing a vision statement is a way of articulating these ideas to yourself, your customers, your employees, and to the world at large.

There is no single format for a vision statement. The statement you decide upon, however, needs to answer the question: 'What will we look like in 10 years time?' Its main purpose is to articulate the 'dream' state of the business. If your business could be everything you dreamed, how would it be?

Here is a famous example of a vision statement:

Bill Gates: 'My vision for Microsoft is that there will be a personal computer on every desk and in every home running Microsoft software.'

Once you have created the long-term vision for your business, it creates the context in which all other decisions are made.

Your statement should stretch expectations, aspirations, and performance.

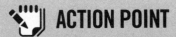

ACTION POINT

To help you to craft your vision statement, try writing your answers to the following questions:

- Pretend it is 10 years in the future and the business is a success. What can you see?

- What has the business become?

- What are you giving your customers?

- What is the biggest change that has taken place?

Creating a mission statement

Mission statements are a way of clearly articulating what you want to do to help you focus your action plan to achieve your vision statement.

Mission statements describe what your business is and precisely what you do. A typical mission statement describes what you do as a business, the products or services you provide and the values you live by.

For any business to succeed, even a business consisting of one individual, it needs to know why it is in business and what it does. The mission statement describes the **what** of your business. It states why your organisation is in business and what you are hoping to achieve.

🔍 EXAMPLE

Dell Computer's mission statement:

'With the power created by Dell Direct and Dell's team of talented people, we are able to provide customers with superb value; high-quality, relevant technology; customized systems; superior service and support; and products and services that are easy to buy and use.'

To break this down:

Dell's purpose is to provide its customers with superb value, high quality technology.

Dell is in the business of selling relevant technology and customised systems to its customers.

Dell's values are that it provides superior service and support, their products are easy to buy, and easy to use.

This mission statement is effective as it clearly states Dell's purpose, the products it provides and the values that drive the business.

A well written vision and mission statement bring all parts of a business together and can influence the behaviour and direction of employees. This has an impact on time management. Just as with the job purpose we described in chapter 4, a good mission statement tells us whether the way we are managing our time is compatible with that mission statement and gives us a sense of direction and a goal to work towards.

Writing a business plan

When I worked for a large organisation in London I was given responsibility for my first budget of just under a million pounds and told I needed to produce a plan for the next financial year. My manager said I needed to see myself as a Managing Director of a medium-sized business and to see him as my bank manager.

In order for me to get the finance I needed to run my department he needed to see a plan. I decided that the best way to prove I needed the finance was to continue to think of my department as a business and come up with a business plan.

If you run a small business, or run a department in a larger organisation, business planning is very important. You will find writing a business plan will help you to be more productive and maximise the use of your time and that of the people who you work with.

The planning cycle can be described as follows:

1. Set objectives

2. Identify resources

3. Produce your plan

4. Implement the plan

5. Review and amend the plan on a regular basis

The plan itself needs to be flexible and to take into account any likely changes in the market, unforeseen factors (such as staff turnover and recruitment) that occur and any other external factors that could affect the achievement of your overall objectives. Once the plan begins to be implemented it needs to be reviewed on a regular basis and changes made to the original plan as circumstances dictate.

TOP TIPS

Remember, business plans cannot be written in stone and need to be flexible enough to deal with those unforeseen circumstances that affect all businesses. You have to make assumptions that may, or may not turn out to be correct. Remember, planning is imperfect, but necessary; not planning is not an option.

What to include in a business plan

Begin by writing down your **objectives**. The plan can cover whatever timescale is appropriate to your situation. Make sure your objectives are SMART (see p.19). Write down objectives that are short, medium and long term.

Next look at your **resources**. Resources need to be included in your plan, as it may be necessary to recruit or bring in additional resources for particular objectives to be met. Resources can include things like funding, equipment, people, knowledge, products, other departments, or external sources of expertise and help.

Next you need to analyse your **market**. A review of the market should include a look at the market now and in the future. What is happening in your marketplace that will influence your plan and the achievement of your objectives?

Next you need to analyse your **products or services**. These can be physical products and services, or the service that you provide internally. If you run an internal department in a company, think about the services you offer. You could be in charge of finance, production, marketing, sales, administration, or logistics. It doesn't matter. You are selling your services either internally or externally. In either case, you have customers to satisfy.

Next you need to have an **activity analysis**. Review what your people need to do to, on a daily, weekly or annual basis to deliver the goods. Do you know how much activity will be required in order for you to achieve your objectives?

Now include a **training plan**. This is a training needs analysis of the individual/team that relates directly to you achieving your objectives. Does the team have the skills it needs to deliver the results that you require?

Next think about your **resources requirements**. Come up with a Cost-Benefit analysis of resources, manpower, equipment, finance etc, required to achieve your business objectives.

TOP TIPS

Cost-Benefit analysis looks at the cost of something and tries to justify that cost by weighing it up against the benefits received. Say for example you want your organisation to buy you a new laptop. To justify the cost, you need to argue the benefits that the investment will bring to the business. If the benefits outweigh the cost it is likely you will get the go ahead to buy the computer.

Finally you need to include an **analysis of your business strategy**. This is the action plan that will deliver what you have promised.

Remember, plans are never 100% accurate and need to be regularly changed and updated. Don't think that because you have come up with one plan you will be able to use it forever. Plans should be reviewed on a regular basis to take account of changing circumstances.

The better the plan, the more efficient you will be and your management of time will be maximised.

PUTTING TOGETHER A LIFE PLAN

A life plan looks at all aspects of your life and that of your family and helps to consolidate your goals and create an action plan for life. There is no one format which suits everyone, but the aim is to look at all aspects of your life and work.

Begin by writing down the aspects of your life that are important to you. We all have choices and it is not my aim to dictate how you should spend your life. It is useful, however, to stop and think and review where you are going and begin to make changes to improve the quality of your life. If you have a partner, or a family, writing a life plan together can be a very rewarding experience.

It can be hard in uncertain times to plan ahead and take a balanced view of where we are in our life. However, during times of uncertainty it can be a very rewarding experience to stop and consider where you are going in your life and start making some plans.

What to include in a life plan

If you do want to take stock of your life then a life plan might help. There are various ways to write a life plan but one popular template contains the following elements:

1. Core values

2. Family goals

3. Financial goals

4. Friends and relatives

5. Work goals

6. Health and fitness goals

7. Relationships

8. Spiritual goals

9. Your relationship with society

Begin by thinking about the **core values** that are most important to you and your family. This could include things like being respectful to others, being polite and caring, treating others with empathy and fairness and trying to give something back to society.

Think about your **goals for your family**. If you have children, you can set your family goals together. If not, you can set your family goals with your partner. Family goals can include anything from the ground rules that you wish to set as a family, to what you do at weekends. It could be as simple as eating one meal every day together, or agreeing how much time you should spend together and what you might like to do as a family in your leisure time. Perhaps you want to learn to ski together, or take regular exercise. Obviously as children get older they may not want to spend as much time with their parents, but then the goals will change as the family gets older. Think about how you currently spend your leisure time. It is so easy to get into bad habits such as crashing out in front of the TV after a hard day at work. Make a list of everything that you each want. This should include all the goals you think you each want to achieve. They may involve money, or material things, or better relationships, or a special vacation, or a change in your personal attitudes or habits.

Think about your **financial goals** for your life. How important is money to you and your family? How much money do you need to earn and what are your goals when you retire from work? How much of your income do you spend and save and what plans have you made for your longer-term financial security? Maybe you always wanted to buy a place in Spain. If it stays as a vague, 'wouldn't it be nice if ...' type of objective it is unlikely it will happen. Once you have written your goals think about how serious you are about achieving them and if you are, go for it.

Think about **friends and relatives**. Do you and your family spend enough time with your friends and relatives who live locally? Are you spending time with friends and relatives who may live somewhere else? Maybe a formal get together is the answer; a summer barbeque, or a big family Christmas.

Next think about your **work goals**. In many families nowadays both spouses have to work and this limits the time we have to spend together. Do you have longer-term work goals that will impact on your life plan? Maybe you would like to change direction and start a family business, or reconsider your current situation and make changes that will give you more time together.

How about your **health and fitness**? How healthy is your current lifestyle? Think about your diet and what you do to keep fit and healthy. How often do you get your health checked? Many of the health problems we face in later life can be reduced with a bit of planning and foresight. Prevention is better than cure and a healthy lifestyle and diet can improve the quality of our lives as we get older. Here is a worrying statistic: in 2007, 24% of adults (aged 16 or over) in England were classified as obese. This represented an overall increase of 15% from 1993. The growing evidence shows that if you are overweight you are more likely to develop health problems, such as heart disease, stroke, diabetes, certain types of cancer and gallbladder disease. Thinking about your health and fitness now can make all the difference in the future.

Relationships should form an important part of your life plan. This is a classic important but not urgent issue, which often gets put to one side. We all need to spend time working on our relationships with spouses, families and friends. By writing a life plan you have the opportunity to reassess the important things in life, and relationships with others is a core issue in having a productive and healthy lifestyle.

There are other issues that you can include in your life plan. These include the **spiritual** side of our lives and our **relationship with society**. How much are we putting back into the community? Many people now do charity work, or give regularly to good causes.

🔍 EXAMPLE

Melvyn Bragg is an author, broadcaster and media personality. He was born in a working class household in Wigton, which is a small market town on the edge of the Lake District, in England. He was educated at Oxford and has had a glittering career in the media. He was asked in an interview how difficult it had been moving from a working class town to a sophisticated London lifestyle as if the latter was more important than the former. He said that where he was brought up, people had very fulfilling lives and did amazingly creative things in their spare time, despite having fairly mundane jobs.

Among other things they bred championship winning racing pigeons, attended debates, sang in choirs, grew their own fruit and vegetables and did all sorts of creative things in their spare time. They also had a great sense of community. He compared this to London society which was shallow and mainly based on money and celebrity. The point to take from this is that you don't need to be wealthy to have a fulfilling lifestyle.

I'm sure none of the people in Wigton actually sat down and worked out their life plans, but they seemed to achieve a well balanced and interesting life despite lacking great financial resources.

So, that is a life plan. If nothing else, sit down with your partner and answer the following three questions. If they make you feel a bit uncomfortable you may want to have a go at producing your own life plan before you do one together.

The questions are:

1. Where am I/are we now?

2. Where do I/we want to be?

3. How am I/are we going to get there?

QUICK RECAP

- *Planning can influence the results we achieve in life and at work.*

- *Planning is a key part of managing your time and identifying your goals.*

- *Planning is an imperfect, but necessary process.*

- *It is important to consider short, medium and long-term goals.*

- *In business an important part of the planning process is to have a vision and a mission statement.*

- *Your business plan should include your objectives, resources, a review of the market, products and service review, an activity analysis, training plan, required resources, and your business strategy.*

- *Your life plan can cover all aspects of a fulfilling life, including your core values and goals for: family, finance, friends and relatives, work, health and fitness, relationships, spirituality and your relationship with society.*

PART 2

TIME MANAGEMENT TOOLS

CHAPTER 6

Using Outlook to manage your time

Microsoft Outlook is the biggest and most used email and diary management program in the world. In this chapter we will look at how you can use Outlook to manage your emails, your diary and hence, your time. We will also look at simple ways of managing contacts and using the Calendar function to produce your time plans.

BASICS OF OUTLOOK

We will start with some basics on how to manage your emails and your time schedule. Computer programs are very frustrating because they have the capability of doing a thousand things but we generally only use 4% or 5% of their potential. But that's okay, if you can understand a few basics that will be enough to improve your time management and get you better organised. This chapter will try to explain the most useful time management features of Outlook in the most simple way possible.

TOP TIPS

For greater insight into what Outlook can do I recommend the Dummies series of books, specifically, *Office 2007 for Dummies*, (John Wiley & Sons) by Wallace Wang. It also gives some great tips on getting the most from Excel, PowerPoint and Access.

Microsoft have developed different versions of Outlook. We have had Outlook '97, '98, 2000, XP, 2003, and 2007 and no doubt new versions will be released in the future. One way to think of these versions, and many other software programs, is to consider they are a bit like your brand new washing machine. You have multiple choices, but only actually use a few key settings.

Most people use Outlook for the basic stuff:

• Sending and receiving emails

• Organising your address book

• Recording appointments

• Reminding you of tasks you need to carry out

• Helping you produce your yearly plan

We will go through these basic functions, and a few more features to make sure you use Outlook to manage your time in the most effective way.

YOUR EMAILS

Volume of emails

Statistics, extrapolations and counting by Radicati Group from October 2008 estimated that in 2008 the number of emails sent per day was around 210 billion. 210 billion messages per day means nearly 2.5 million emails are sent every second. About 70% to 72% (or between 128 and 132 billion) of them might be spam and viruses. The genuine emails are sent by around 33 billion users.

You can imagine the effect this has on the time management of people who need to access and send emails as part of their job. Although emails started in the mid 60s it was only in 1993 when AOL connected their system to the internet that email became global. Nowadays we are in danger of being ruled by the constant flow of information that comes in and out of our computers.

TOP TIPS

It's estimated that 95% of emails are spam. It's essential you get a good spam filter to get rid of these, or at least put them somewhere else so they are not clogging up your inbox.

Dealing with emails

One of the most basic time management techniques is to set aside blocks of time to do tasks like phoning, having meetings and dealing with administration. This prevents us from flitting from one job to another out of boredom, or lack of direction. It's also important to manage your inbox. Here are a few key actions you can take to help you deal with your emails.

First of all **download a spam management programme**. These programs transfer spam to a separate folder that you can look at when you have some time and delete the stuff you don't want to keep.

Next, **think about the emails you receive**. Most of what you receive is called *reference information*. In other words you don't need to take action, but the information could be useful to you at some point. Set up a series of file folders in your email system, so you can transfer these emails to the appropriate file for future reference.

The rest of your emails will **require action**, so we can think about how to manage these.

When you access your emails think about setting priorities. Deal with the urgent stuff first, in other words, tasks that have a time deadline. Look at the important and not urgent stuff next. If you can't begin working on these now, schedule time into your calendar when you can begin working on them. Do the not important, not urgent stuff in your own time, or just don't do them.

Follow these five steps to deal with every kind of email you receive:

1. **Delete it**: Get rid of stuff you don't need.

2. **Do it**: Take action now and get it out of the way. Once it is done file it away somewhere other than your inbox if you need to keep a record of the email.

3. **Delegate it**: If it is appropriate give it to someone else then file it away, or record a future action if necessary.

4. **Defer it**: Leave it till later. Make a note on your calendar for future action.

Here are a few more key tips to getting on top of your inbox:

1. Schedule time to process emails. It is naïve to think we don't want to keep looking at our emails, so be realistic. I try to limit myself to once an hour, which still isn't perfect. If you have more strength of character you may be able to limit it to twice, or three times a day.

2. You can filter your emails by date, subject or who it came from. How you manage this depends on the volume of traffic you receive. The easiest way is just start from the top and work down.

TOP TIPS

You can set up rules in Outlook that mean certain emails are sent directly to a designated folder, or are automatically forwarded to a colleague. This can be useful for dealing with email that you are copied into. By creating a CC folder and a rule that all CC emails go there, you can free up time by only checking this every few days, and meaning the only emails in your inbox are directly for your attention.

3. The preview pane in Outlook allows you to view your emails without opening them. This means you can delete stuff more quickly. Make sure you use it!

4. Finally, if you receive a lot of emails build time into your schedule to clean up your files and get rid of the stuff you don't need. It is no different from having a session cleaning out your filing cabinet. Find a time when you are not busy and just do it.

Email distraction

Email can be a great distraction from the work you need to get done when you check it constantly and allow it to interrupt you. To properly manage your time, try not to look into your inbox every five minutes, or respond to the ping and pop up box that appears when an email arrives. Most messages are not urgent and **can** wait. As mentioned previously build some time into your schedule for checking and replying to your emails whether it's once an hour or a few times a day; for example set aside 30 minutes at the beginning, middle and end of the day to look at and respond to emails. Don't let it control your time.

TOP TIPS

In Outlook you can remove the email pop up and the pinging noise that tells you a new email has arrived. It has been calculated that 75% of the emails we receive are rubbish, but it takes on average 64 seconds to deal with each email.

 ACTION POINT

To remove the sound and visual icon when you receive an email go to:

Mail
↓
Options
↓
Email options
↓
Advanced email options
↓

Now you can untick the boxes that say 'When new items arrive in my inbox play a sound', 'briefly change the mouse cursor', and 'show an envelope icon in the notification area'

Hey presto! No more annoying sounds and notifications.

Sending emails

If you are sending emails there are some basics to help you save time and be more productive.

Keep it simple

Make sure your message is clear and that the people you send your email to really need to receive it. Keep it as brief as possible.

Informality

Nowadays people are less worried about formality. If in doubt be more formal, but words like 'Hi' and 'Regards' are usually quite acceptable if you know the recipient, or have communicated in the past.

Try not to use text speak

'UR important' may be okay in some circumstances, but may not be appropriate for a business message.

Grammar counts

Grammar, punctuation and spelling are important and very easy to check in Outlook. It takes very little time and says a lot about your professionalism. Click Tools/Spelling and Grammar to do a quick spell and grammar check.

Don't be too emotional

Never send an email if you are angry. Also, avoid using capital letters to make a point. This is the email version of shouting. The best thing, if you are not sure, is to write your email, store it as a draft and come back to it the next day.

Can you phone?

Sometimes it is quicker to phone. Think about it. Do you need an official record of your correspondence?

Use CC & BCC wisely

Be careful who you copy into the email. Consider who really needs to read your email. If you can set parameters within your teams about why and when you copy people in, you'll quickly notice a reduction in irrelevant emails. If you need someone to see your email privately use the BCC, blind copy option. Open a new email and double click on the CC option. This then enables you to send a blind copy (BCC).

Don't ask for confirmation

Resist asking everyone to acknowledge receipt of your email. It annoys people and just creates more traffic. Also, avoid marking every email as top priority.

As with all the time management tips in this book, have a think about how much time you spend sending and reading emails. Emails keep us busy, but do they make us more productive? Always keep in mind that working harder isn't necessarily the same as working smarter.

YOUR CONTACTS

Most of us have personal and business contacts and your PC is the best place to store this information. Prior to the PC it was recorded manually in a diary or a Rolodex system and there was a limit on how the information could be used. Now we can print off lists, labels, reminders and To Do lists at the press of a button.

Here is how you store contact information:

1. Open up Outlook

2. Click on Contacts

3. Click on File

4. Click on New Contact

This opens up a window and you can store a host of information on your contact, whether it is a business or personal contact.

Information you can input includes:

- Name
- Job title
- Company
- Home address
- Business address
- Email address
- Web address
- Phone numbers:
  - Home
  - Business
  - Mobile
  - Fax

Inputting data is the boring bit, but once you have finished it will save you lots of time in the future. Once you have your data on your computer you can begin to manage the information for producing lists, labels and prompts and reminders.

Grouping your contacts

In Outlook you can easily create a distribution list of contacts. This is a group of email addresses that is added to your address book as a single contact. When you send a message it goes to everyone on the list. This saves time when you send regular emails to the same group of people.

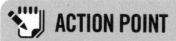 **ACTION POINT**

To set this up click File/New/Distribution List.

Click Select Members.

Highlight the email addresses you want to appear on the list and give the list a name, by typing this in the name box.

Click Save and Close.

The distribution list will be found as a separate entry on your address list.

Searching for contacts or emails

Searching for contacts is easy. If you just want to send an email open *Mail* and click the *New* button. This opens a blank email. Begin to type the name of your contact in the To: box and Outlook will produce a list of names that match. When you see the name you want, click on that name and the email address will appear in the To: box.

To search for a specific contact click on *Contacts* and you will see a search bar at the top of the screen that says *Look for.* Type in the name of the contact you are looking for, or part of the name and click *Find now* and a range of options will be displayed.

To search for a specific email you have sent or received, go to the folder at the left hand side of the screen that you want to search; in my Outlook these are Inbox, Sent items, Deleted items, Junk mail and Spam but these may be different depending on the version you are using.

Set up folders for specific clients or projects for which you receive a lot of emails. This makes it easier to search the system and keep track of things. Set up a folder with the client's name or the name of the project.

So, if you are looking for an email you sent, open the *Sent* folder and search for the email. Put the name of the person you are looking for, or the title of the email and click *Find*. Outlook will display a list of your contacts and ones with similar names and you can click on the email you were looking for.

SETTING TASKS AND TO DO LISTS

Using the 'To Do list' function in Outlook 2007 or the tasks and calendar function in Outlook 2003 is a great way of reducing the amount of emails you store in your inbox. They both allow you to choose when you'll deal with an email and store the email in a task/To Do list for that allocated time, with an automatic reminder function.

This is great for managing your time. You drag an individual email to the tasks folder and it allows you to set a time and date when you can deal with the email. This means the email is removed from your inbox until you want to deal with it. It stops you checking and reading the same email every time you go to your inbox – a bad time management habit!

The *To Do* bar in Outlook 2007 shows items to do for that day and features a calendar and a list of tasks. It can be displayed on the right hand side of the screen in different formats. To open the To Do bar click *View/ To Do bar/Normal* or *Minimised*.

The benefit of this function is that your To Do list is written for you; saving time and effort on your behalf. You spend less time organising your emails, or searching through a long list to find what you really need.

Outlook 2003 is a bit more complicated. Here you create a task by clicking the task button on the left hand side of the screen. Click *New* on the toolbar at the top of the screen and fill in the details of your task. You can type in information on the due date, status, priority, percentage of the task completed, reminders and notes. Every time you click on tasks it will display the full list of the tasks you need to complete.

You can also set a reminder by dragging an email to the Tasks box on the left hand side of the screen. This opens a new window and you can ask Windows to remind you when a particular task needs to be carried out.

USING THE OUTLOOK CALENDAR

The Outlook calendar is no different to the calendar you stick behind the kitchen door, only it can do so much more. Outlook can manage your calendar and remind you of what you need to be doing. There are a multitude of functions if you want to find them all: what follows are the basics that will help you the most in achieving your time management goals. You will also find there are different ways of achieving the same objective.

The calendar is designed to manage your time looking at four different types of entry:

1. Appointments made on a specific day with an estimated time that involve you and others outside your organisation.

2. Meetings that involve others in your organisation.

3. All day events that take up the whole day.

4. Tasks that may, or may not need a scheduled timescale.

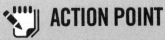 **ACTION POINT**

To access the calendar, click *Calendar* in the navigation pane, or click a day in the calendar on the To Do bar.

If it is an **appointment**, click on the desired time and type in the details of the appointment.

For a **meeting** entry, click on the time and right click on the new meeting tab. Fill in the details of the meeting and the details of those who will be attending. Outlook will send an email to attendees with details of the meeting.

For a **task**, double click on the relevant day and fill in details of the task. This can have a scheduled start and end time. Outlook will send you a reminder depending on how you set the reminder tag. This can be anything from five minutes to two weeks before the appropriate task, or meeting.

Outlook is a very flexible calendar. It can do exactly what you want. It is a diary that records events and sends out reminders prior to the event taking place. Using the calendar will save you time by automatically emailing attendees and putting the date in their diaries, as well as allowing you to drag any relevant emails and store them in the appointment for easy reference. It also allows you to check people's availability by looking at the times they have booked in their diaries. (However, this only works if all colleagues use the online calendar and keep it up to date.)

 TOP TIPS

Your Outlook calendar can be synchronised with other electronic devices such as a phone, Blackberry or PDA. This means you have access to an up-to-date calendar whether at your desk or on the road and means you only have to enter something once.

TIME PLANS USING OUTLOOK

When you put together weekly, monthly or annual plans there are certain things to remember. One is to be sensible and to leave sufficient space for unplanned events. Another is to build in time for those important but not urgent tasks that mean everything to the effective time manager. Another is to schedule time in the diary so you can respond to emails that come into your inbox.

Many incoming emails can be dealt with fairly quickly, but some require more action and need a slot in the diary. Finally, there are some events that recur weekly or monthly that you can put in the diary once and forget about them. Setting recurring appointments or tasks can help set up a time plan to follow.

Q EXAMPLE

In chapter 4 we looked at prioritising tasks. When I sit down to plan my year I begin by listing my goals. At this stage I am most concerned about the important stuff. These can then be classed as important and urgent, which means there is a time deadline and important and not urgent tasks, where a time deadline doesn't exist; yet!

Here are some examples:

Important and Urgent

Send out monthly newsletter to the people on my database on 20th of each month.

Write one article per month to distribute on the internet on 1st of each month.

Run a weekly three hour prospecting session every Monday.

Produce my VAT records on the last Thursday in each quarter.

Go through my inbox each morning at 8.30 and take action on any emails that require it.

Leave every Friday free to do essential administration.

Important and Not Urgent

Review my website.

Research new ways to market my business.

Write another book.

Research sources of funding for training.

Learn how to speak Spanish.

I can now use Outlook features to come up with a timeplan and set reminders to help me complete my tasks.

 ACTION POINT

Click on the *Calendar* icon in the left hand pane. Double click on the *Date* you want the first recurring event to take place. Fill in the other details for the event; including the subject, location, start and end time, reminder and any other details. Click the *Recurrence* button, fill in the recurrence details and click OK. Click save and close.

Other events can be manually placed into the calendar by clicking *View day* and highlighting the time you want to set aside. Type in the details of the event and it will be put in your calendar.

Using recurring events

If you receive an email that requires attention later and you want to schedule this into your calendar, just drag the email over to the calendar icon in the left hand pane and this will open a window that you can complete and the email details will appear in the calendar and can be forgotten about until the appropriate day.

What this enables you to do to is print off your daily, weekly or monthly schedule, or view it on your screen. Personally, I like to have a paper copy in front of me on my desk for each day and I stick my monthly plans on the office wall, however you may find it easiest to refer to your electronic version.

Remember, no plan is perfect. Outlook is a very comprehensive software program and in this chapter we have really just looked at some basics that you can use to help manage your time. There is a lot more you can do if you are willing to investigate Outlook in more detail.

The key points are to schedule time for the important and urgent and the important, not urgent stuff and leave some time for the unplanned events that go with every job.

OUTLOOK ALTERNATIVES

For the sake of balance there are alternatives to Outlook that you can use. While I use Outlook and it gives me all I need to manage my emails and my diary, here are some alternatives you may wish to check out:

- Apple mail
- Qualcomm Eudora 8 Beta
- Novell Evolution 2
- Google Gmail
- Novell GroupWise8
- KMail (Linux KDE)
- IBM Lotus notes 8.5
- Mozilla Thunderbird 2 with Sunbird
- Microsoft Windows Mail
- Yahoo Zimbra

A lot of these alternative systems look very similar and have very similar features. The key is to find a system you feel comfortable with and decide exactly what you want it to do for you.

KEEP IT SIMPLE

The problem with all software is that because it can do so many things it is difficult to pull out the really important stuff that can be used easily by your average PC user. Use the KISS principle: Keep it simple (stupid!). By creating folders, using your calendar and the To Do list function you can turn your overwhelming inbox into something useful and manageable. Make sure you build some time into your schedule to maintain your database. For more information buy an Office manual or search the internet for online tutorials and tips. The best thing to do is learn enough for your needs, keep it simple and keep it up to date.

QUICK RECAP

- *Apply the same principles of managing your emails as you do to managing your time.*

- *Schedule time for dealing with incoming emails.*

- *When you send emails make sure you don't copy everyone in. Ask yourself: is the email relevant to each recipient?*

- *Is it as easy to phone the person involved, or go and speak to them?*

- *Manage your contacts. A little effort up front saves time later.*

- *Group contacts as required and this gives a single email address for the group.*

- *Produce a To Do list daily and weekly.*

- *Use the calendar function to manage your meetings, appointments and tasks.*

- *Use Outlook to produce your time plans with reminders and recurring events pre-programmed into your diary.*

CHAPTER 7

Dealing with interruptions

One of the main causes of time management problems at work is having to deal with interruptions. In this chapter we will explore the different causes of interruptions at work and look at several strategies for dealing with them. We will look at why we get interrupted, different sources of interruption, how to delegate more effectively and how to get more control of your working environment.

SOURCES OF INTERRUPTION

Interruptions can be a constant source of irritation for people at work. It hasn't been helped by the open plan nature of most offices today. People are easily accessible and it can be difficult to work on a project that requires quiet concentration and an uninterrupted period of time.

Sources of interruptions are often co-workers and telephone calls. However, we also have email interruptions, as we discussed in the previous chapter, where people are constantly accessing their inbox and being notified of new email as it arrives. Other sources of interruptions can be external noise, but you also need to aware of the danger of self-interruptions, where we break off from the task in hand and start tackling another job, often with a lower priority.

It doesn't matter how well organised you are, if your manager asks to see you, or a colleague drops in for a chat it can waste a lot of time and reduce your productivity at work.

🔍 EXAMPLE

I once worked for a client who was a Sales Director who operated an open door policy. He had an office with a door guarded by a secretary, but he got it into his head that to be an effective manager he needed to be constantly available to his team. He was a really nice guy who was very popular with his team, but who found it very hard to delegate. He would talk to individual salespeople as well as the managers who reported to him. The problem was that his phone was ringing at regular intervals during the day and he had a stream of people dropping in to give him their problems to sort out. He asked me for my advice on what to do and I said we would begin by gathering some evidence.

We produced an interruptions log. He was usually at work at 8.00am and the phone would be ringing shortly afterwards. On the interruptions log I got him to record:

- *The time of the interruption*
- *The duration*
- *Type of interruption; visit, phone call*
- *The reason for the interruption*
- *The outcome of the interruption*
- *Finally a section that asked 'Could this person have solved this problem themselves?'*

We monitored his schedule for a week and then did an analysis of the results. What we found was:

- *60% of the interruptions were from salespeople with a problem they could have solved themselves, or could have given to their manager.*

- *Calls came in at regular intervals during the day making it difficult for him to do tasks that required periods of concentration.*

- *25% of the calls that came in were on issues that could have been dealt with by his secretary. For example, companies ringing in to cold sell products and services.*

- *15% of the calls were necessary and required his attention.*

I felt there were three main problems here. One was his inability to say no, the other was his unwillingness to delegate and the third was his open door.

To fix these problems we began with his secretary. I took her through the interruptions log and we decided which of the calls should be dealt with by her and simply not put through. She was a resource he just wasn't using.

Next we met with his managers and agreed some basic ground rules. Again by analysing his interruptions log we identified a range of issues that could be more sensibly dealt with by his managers and they were told in future the sales team would use the manager as the first point of call.

We then shut his door. From then on the deal with his team was that they could call him between 8.00am and 9.00am and 5.00pm and 6.00pm as those were the times when his door was open. If there was an urgent problem he would take the call, but this would be monitored and policed.

He looked a bit panicky at this point and said to me 'But what will I do with all that free time?' The answer was that he would have now time to do his real job, which was to direct and not manage the sales team. Managing the team was what he paid his managers for.

DELEGATION

Delegation is an important skill for managers to learn. In the above example our sales director was failing to make the most of his team and by delegating he freed up his time to do what he was paid to do; to lead the team.

Avoiding delegation

People often don't delegate because it can seem easier just to do the job rather than give someone else the skills to do it. People like to feel busy and often it feels good to regress to your previous job before they promoted you. In the previous example the sales director had regressed back into the role of sales manager, because it felt more comfortable

Why delegate?

Delegation develops people's skills and frees up time for you to do the more important stuff. It will enable you to look at your own schedule and start working on more of the important, non-urgent tasks that really matter.

The most effective managers know the power of delegation. Think about some of our leaders of industry. Richard Branson couldn't run his Virgin business empire alone. He has built a team around him to achieve his objectives and his role has been to provide vision and direction to his management team.

The starting point here is to have a very clear vision of where you are going and how you are going to get there. Delegation involves risk, but, given the right person and by delegating wisely, you can achieve more than if you work alone. Delegation is not abdication. It requires a lot of hands on support at the beginning. However, once the person is confident you can let them get on with it.

To delegate well you have to be clear about what you want them to achieve, set clearly defined standards of performance and have systems in place for monitoring and measuring performance.

TOP TIPS

TOP TIPS ON DELEGATING

1. Choose your delegate wisely. Do they have the capability to take on more responsibility?

2. Give very clear objectives on what you want to be achieved and the standards of performance that are required.

3. Don't just delegate the worst jobs.

4. Monitor performance quite closely at first while the person learns to do the new tasks.

5. Give feedback and praise good performance.

6. Be patient. People need to learn new skills and may not be as good as you at first.

CHANGE THE WAY YOU SEE INTERRUPTIONS

It is rare that an interruption is both important and urgent. Depending on the time of day and your work schedule, minor interruptions can either be dealt with straight away, or left until a more convenient time. Try not to be the sort of person who automatically drops everything to deal with a minor matter at the expense of more important work.

You also need to see interruptions in the context of your job. Are interruptions a part of your job? If you have a job in customer services or in any working environment where people need a quick response, that is the nature of the job and you need to begin to plan accordingly.

Many interruptions are manageable with a bit of forward planning. If you are a manager and have regular contact with members of your team, schedule time in the diary when it is a more convenient time to talk and try to deal with problems or issues in batches, rather than one at a time.

TOP TIPS

Many problems reoccur so it can be very useful to have a common approach within the team for dealing with them. It is good to reassess ways we have typically dealt with recurring problems. Comments like 'this is the way we have always done it' should be challenged. We need to constantly reassess our working methods and how we deal with common problems in order to avoid the same problems delaying your work over and over again.

Try to stay focused on the task in hand and worry about the interruption later. If you are going to deal with the interruption later on explain what you are doing and why. People are usually quite happy to give you some leeway if they understand what is going to happen and when.

It is quite acceptable, when you are interrupted, to ask the other person how long the interruption will take and to challenge whether you are the best person to deal with the situation that has arisen.

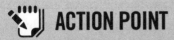

ACTION POINT

Set up an interruptions log to work out the main source of your interruptions. Make a list and then look at the techniques for dealing with interruptions below to find the one to help you.

TECHNIQUES FOR DEALING WITH INTERRUPTIONS

In an open plan office

Many people work in an open plan environment where the traditional style of office has been replaced by open plan desks. Open planning was sold on the basis that it improved communications and got rid of the hierarchical barriers that used to exist. While some people thrive on the buzz of a busy office, others find it difficult to concentrate, get constantly interrupted, are distracted by background noise and feel they are constantly being monitored.

If you find it hard to complete work that requires privacy and peace and quiet in a busy, noisy open plan office there are various techniques to try. Wearing earphones to block out noise can be useful. Whether or not you are listening to music it also sends a signal to people that you are busy which will reduce interruptions. Other options include booking a meeting room to work in when you really need to concentrate or working at home if you are able.

Another technique is to use visual signs to indicate you are busy and can't be interrupted. This could be as simple as a red flag for 'busy don't interrupt', and green for available, or the more blunt 'go away' sign that a colleague of mine used. If you find you are constantly interrupted by people you manage, you'll need to look again at the way you communicate and whether you have enough regular and frequent meetings. Consider whether you can establish certain times in the day when you are free to be interrupted, and other times in which you can work uninterrupted. It's also useful to get together as a team and work out strategies for dealing with these problems.

Common interruptions

Here are some regular scenarios and some thoughts on how to deal with them.

People dropping by

Someone walks into the office or up to your desk and you are in the middle of an important piece of work. Stand up, if you can walk away from your desk and walk towards them and stand and talk with them. Don't give them the chance to sit down and get comfortable if the interruption is fairly trivial.

If it turns out to be important and requires some time right now, you can sit them down, but try to set some sort of time deadline, based on what else you have to do and the relative importance of the two tasks.

Customer complaints

You have a complaining customer on the phone. The worst thing you can do is to try and solve their problem when they are angry or frustrated. The best way to handle them is to listen to them, try not interrupt, show empathy and use a technique of issuing NCGs (non-committal grunts) over the phone. This way, after a few minutes their anger will subside and they will usually apologise and say they realise it isn't your fault. This is a sign that they have got most of their anger out of the way and you can then begin to talk with them logically. This method is very successful and saves a lot of time on the phone.

Too many phone calls

Using voicemail can give you a break from being interrupted by phone. If you do get regular interruptions by phone you can block off some time during the day when the phone is switched to voicemail.

The good thing here is that when you do go to answer your voicemails, they are all together and can be handled quickly and efficiently. But remember you do need a fall back position so that if the MD needs to talk with you urgently there is a way of being contacted, say by mobile, rather than the office landline.

Chatty co-workers

You may have a co-worker who likes to chat a lot. Usually this is fairly trivial stuff, but you don't want to upset them. People like this can be real time wasters. You worry about upsetting them, but they are stopping you doing your work. I personally feel it pays to be blunt and honest, and offer an alternative time for a brief chat when you are not busy. You could say something like: 'John, I am very keen to hear about your new vegetable garden, but I have to finish this report for Sarah in the next hour. Why don't I come and find you when I have finished and we can have five minutes then. Anyway, I must keep going with this.' You can then resume work and avoid eye contact. There is no need to be rude, but you have the right not to be interrupted over trivial matters.

As mentioned above, another technique you can try is to find a hiding place where you can work interrupted such as a meeting room or local coffee shop. Talk to your manager. They may even let you do some uninterrupted work at home.

Manager interruptions

Your manager asks you to work on another project, despite having told you your current project should take precedence. It is important not to give in too easily here. If you agree too easily it will happen again. Ask questions. Why the change of priority? Have they thought through the consequences? What about the current project? It is okay to negotiate when this kind of thing happens. The problem is that if your manager is the sort of person who chops and changes their mind it can have disastrous consequences on you and other members of your team. See p.53 for advice on how to reconcile your different working techniques and manage your manager.

Emails

This is looked at in more detail in chapter 6, but the simplest ways to avoid email becoming a distraction is to turn off the pop up and ping noise which happens when you receive an email. See p.78 on how to turn this feature off.

Copied into emails

Another problem with emails can be if you are unnecessarily copied in on everything, taking you away from what you are working on. This is a tough one to manage. A client of mine in Leeds tried to stop this happening and emailed all the staff for their comments generating an avalanche of electronic traffic. The best way to handle this is to get together with members of the team and work out some rules for copying people on email. Then stick to them. If you are regularly copied in to emails that are not relevant, ask the person sending them to remove you from the list.

LEARNING HOW TO SAY NO

One important part of managing interruptions is being able to say no. In chapter 10 we will cover techniques for being more assertive and why it is important but for now we will look at the simple task of being able to say 'no'. We say 'yes' to other people because we want to please them. But eventually when we can't continue to deliver, we let them down and we feel guilty. Both parties suffer. It is this need to please people that causes the problems associated with saying no.

If you have a plan you must try and stick to it. For example if someone asks you to sell adverts into a newspaper say 'I have already decided to focus on internet marketing so press and magazine adverts are not what we are looking for.' If they persist stay calm and repeat yourself. This technique used to be called 'broken record' in an era when records used to stick and you heard the same line over and over.

TOP TIPS

It is sometimes useful though to find out if you are being asked to do something extra. Ask questions to find out just how big a job it is. It may not take long and agreeing to do it might give you brownie points with your boss.

Remember that you have a right to say no. Remember that others may take you for granted and even lose respect for you if you don't. Practice makes perfect. Try out some non-threatening situations first. Be polite, but firm in saying no. You only build false hopes with vague responses. For instance, the phrase 'I'll try to be there' in response to a party invitation is giving yourself an excuse to avoid a commitment. It doesn't do anyone any favours. Look for alternatives. This is called 'no to go', in other words 'I can't make it tonight, but I am sure I can free up one night next week. How does that sound?'

Eye contact is very important when saying no. It shows you are confident and mean what you say.

TOP TIPS

When you have to say yes

Sometimes, saying no is simply unavoidable. It just doesn't work to say no every time you are asked to do something. Sometimes you have to say yes but make sure you have the confidence to look after your rights as an individual.

Here are some techniques to use when you *have* to say yes:

- Tell the person you can agree to their request this time, but ask how you might plan better for the next time.

- Tell them yes, but remind them they owe you one. For example, they might cover for you next time you need time off.

- Tell them yes, but set the timetable yourself. Give a realistic deadline that will enable you to complete the job to a high standard and on time.

QUICK RECAP

- *Understand your sources of interruptions and answer the question: 'Is it part of my job to deal with interruptions?'*

- *Try managing your interruptions by producing an interruptions log and analysing the results to find ways to avoid these interruptions in the future.*

- *Learn to delegate.*

- *Try to find time for uninterrupted work if this is important in helping you achieve your goals.*

- *Find a hiding place where you can work undisturbed.*

- *Decide if the next interruption can be dealt with quickly and put out of the way, or does it need scheduled time to sort it out.*

- *Build interruption time into your time plan.*

- *Learn how to say no and when to say yes.*

CHAPTER 8

Essential time management skills

In this chapter we will look at some of the key skills that you can develop in order to be a better time manager. One of the greatest sources of time management problems is that we put off unpleasant tasks and this causes trouble, not just for ourselves, but also for those who work with us. We will see why we procrastinate and look at some ways of reducing its effects. We will also look at how we manage our workspace, both on our computer and in the office. Finally, we will look at decision-making and the effective use of the telephone; all of which is designed to make life easier and more productive.

PROCRASTINATION

Procrastination happens when we put off tackling a particular task and leave it till a later date. This often happens because we get anxious about starting or completing certain tasks, or making decisions that we don't feel confident about. Procrastination means putting things off until tomorrow and has been called 'the thief of time'.

When we procrastinate we risk personal stress and the disapproval of others as time deadlines are missed. We all procrastinate to some degree and sometimes get away with it, but for some people it can be a real psychological problem. Putting things off can provide a bit of temporary relief, but problems tend not to go away and decisions need to be made. There are several reasons why we procrastinate:

1. The task we face seems too difficult and we lack the confidence to take it on.

2. We worry about the disapproval of others if we fail to complete the task.

3. We don't have the necessary skills to do the task well.

4. Our objectives are unclear and the timescales are vague.

TOP TIPS

When you have a task to complete and you are not looking forward to starting it the best strategy can be to tackle it early in the day, or even better, straight away. Things often turn out to be not as bad as we expected and by getting them out of the way early, it gets rid of the stress of anticipation that we experience when putting off something unpleasant to a later date.

🔍 EXAMPLE

As a salesperson I was never keen on cold calling because of the amount of rejection I received from people who were not interested in talking to me. I would have a list of potential clients in front of me and would sit and stare at it. Then of course I needed a coffee. Also, I had to have a word with my manager before starting and there was that report that I needed to write… and so it went on. I was having a conversation with myself trying to convince me that there were other things I should be doing. We used to call it 'the thousand tonne phone'. Impossible to lift up and use, so it stayed where it was.

There is only one answer. Get started. Take a deep breath, pick the phone up and dial. I even remember putting off ringing one of my best customers one day, which wasn't a cold call, and having the conversation with myself. 'He'll not be in'; 'they are probably not going to be interested' and so on. When I eventually rang the guy his first words were 'I'm glad you rang Frank. We were just talking about you the other day and need to discuss doing some more training'. This just goes to show that procrastinating not only adds to our stress levels as we approach deadlines but can also mean we miss out on opportunities by delaying.

Tips to beat procrastination

Whether you do it on your PC or on a piece of paper make a list of what needs to get done. This can be listed in no particular order at first, and will give you a handle on just what you need to accomplish that day, or that week.

Your daily list should show you the meetings, appointments and tasks you need to achieve for the day. In chapter 6 we discussed using Outlook, but if you are not into computers and prefer using bits of paper, keep lists for each day preferably on the same sheet of paper, showing all your intended activities and a scheduled time for each if possible. Producing an effective To Do list also links in to goal setting (see p.18) and setting priorities (see p.45).

Here are some tips on making lists:

- Make a random listing of everything you would like to accomplish during the day. Then go through the list, numbering everything in order of priority. Probably the most value from this form of listing will come from you completing the items you marked 1 and 2. Make sure you schedule specific blocks of time to do both of them.

- Do not schedule secondary items, just plan to do them as time permits. You need flexibility to handle the unexpected events of the day.

- The danger of the To Do list is that it tends to be based upon urgency. So always take a moment when preparing your list to see if the things you plan to do are going to make a direct contribution to the purpose and goals of your job and yourself. Most people don't manage to get to the bottom of their list by the end of the day. Don't worry. If you've worked according to your priorities, then you will have done the important things for that day. This is what time management is all about!

- You can produce a list for your daily, weekly, monthly, or annual goals. The same principles apply to each. Brainstorm your goals, rewrite them in order of importance then schedule time to begin working on them.

TOP TIPS

If you find yourself transferring an item more than twice to your new list ask yourself 'am I managing my time or just writing lists?'

- Spend the last few minutes of each day preparing your list for the next day. This is one of the most effective time management practices. Last thing, you usually write a more demanding and complete list. If you leave it until the morning, the pressure of events can cause the list-making to be haphazard or the priority setting to be based solely on urgency and not importance.

- If you have a big project that needs doing begin some work on it now. Plan how you break the overall objective down into a series of smaller objectives.

- If you have some stuff to do that won't take very long just do it now. It can be very psychologically rewarding to achieve a lot of things in a relatively short space of time. There are no hard and fast rules for managing your time. Do what works for you, but understand, the basics to remember are:

1. Have a plan.

2. Tackle one thing at a time.

3. Do the important stuff as well as the urgent.

4. Don't be hard on yourself. You cannot manage your time all the time.

MANAGING YOUR DESK

The principles behind organising your time electronically and physically are very similar. By the same token, the principles behind managing the flow of paper in our workplace and managing the flow of electronic information are also very similar. We need systems in place for controlling the flow of information and storing it for future reference and easy access.

We all have different jobs and will therefore need to set up different filing systems. The key point to remember is you need to analyse how information flows into your work space. We receive information by mail, email, fax and telephone calls. Records need to be kept and information stored if it needs to be accessed in the future, or if there is a legal requirement to keep a record.

To set up a filing system, look at the flow of information into your office. Certain things require action now, others require action at a later date, while others need to be kept for the record and may need to be accessed later. For example, I split my filing system between work requiring action and work that needs to be stored.

Your workspace and paper

One of the best time management tips you can use is to have a clear desk so you can work on one thing at a time. Set up an in-tray that gets regularly filtered and a series of paper files, relating to your business, in a small filing cabinet.

A simple filing system that is streamlined and orderly will support you in getting your job done. Try to make your desk a clean working surface that helps you to focus your energy on the task in hand.

It can be useful to begin by drawing a map of where everything should go, based on the flow of paper within your office. When you receive an email it goes into your inbox. When paper comes into your workspace you need a parking place where everything goes when it arrives. This might be an in-tray, or another type of file.

When paper arrives into your office there are a limited number of actions that can be taken:

- Take action straight away. Depending on your priorities for the day you may be able to deal with this at once.

- Take action later today. Park the paper in the in-tray and schedule some time to complete the task.

- Take action at a later date. Set up a diary dating file.

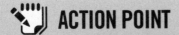 **ACTION POINT**

To set up a diary dating file divide the file into 43 sections; 31 sections for days in the current month and 12 sections; one for each month of the year. So, everything for the current month is filed in the relevant day it requires action. Everything for future months is filed in that relevant month. At the beginning of each new month take the pages out of that month's section and distribute them to the relevant day section so they can be pulled out at the beginning of each day for action to be taken.

- File it. Have a separate in tray for items to be filed. This is not urgent and can be done when you have a bit of spare time. Try to do this once a week or delegate it if possible.

 TOP TIPS Think about the type of paperwork you receive and create and make sure you have appropriate files for each major area. For example, in your filing cabinet you could have a place for the paperwork connected to current projects, customer files and other paperwork connected to the business, including bank statements, insurance policies, and all the paraphernalia that goes with running a business.

Everyone's system will be different depending on the job they do. To manage the flow of paper, as you do with the flow of electronic information:

1. Do it now

OR

2. Delegate it

OR

3. File it for future action and schedule the time when you will deal with it

OR

4. Get rid of it (shred, delete) unless you need to keep a paper copy

For paperwork that has been sent for your information such as trade magazines, mailshots etc, create a dump drawer and go through this when and if you have the time.

USING THE TELEPHONE

Using the telephone can be a great time waster or an equally good time saving device – depending on the skill of the user. With incoming calls we are at the mercy of the person calling. If you find phone calls are high on your interruptions log (p.97) and you don't have an assistant to filter your calls, here are some options you can try:

- Use voicemail during busy times when you don't wish to be disturbed. On voicemail, give your email address as a potential method of alternative contact.

- Switch off your mobile during meetings unless you are waiting for an urgent call. Yes, I know this is obvious, but, apart from it being rude when a phone goes off during a meeting, your bad time management habits affect those around you.

- Let people know when you are most likely to be available. Be polite, but firm with unsolicited sales calls. If you are busy, say so and arrange an alternative time.

- When you are making outgoing calls try to set aside a block of time when they can all be done at once. This is a much more efficient way of making calls than doing them individually as it will focus your mind and so save time. Set yourself objectives for each call and try to minimise the amount of time spent on each call. Have any relevant documents to hand and some means of taking notes during the call itself.

- It can be difficult when dealing with people who want to chat. They can be major time wasters. Without being rude, at some point you need to make it clear why you are calling and get down to business. Wait till they have finished a sentence then say something like: 'That's really interesting John. I have a meeting I have to go to in 10 minutes. Can we discuss your staff problems now and I will see what I can do to sort them out today. Is that okay?' In other words be assertive, give a reason for moving from social chat to business and get their agreement.

MAKING DECISIONS

If you are a manager, or you are faced with having to make a decision, it is quite useful to know the different types of decision-making open to you. The type of decision you make will have an impact on your time management and that of others.

There are three basic types of decision-making:

1. **Autocratic**: this is where you make a decision yourself based on facts you already know.

2. **Consultative**: this is where you consult with others to get their ideas and opinions, but in the end you still make the decision yourself.

3. **Group**: this is where a group of people make a decision, and each member of the group has an equal say.

 ACTION POINT

Let's assume you are the manager of a team. Imagine if, from today, every decision you made was **autocratic**. What would be the impact on the speed of decision-making and how would it impact on the quality of the decision and the morale of your team?

Now imagine if, from today, every decision you made was **consultative**. What would be the impact on the speed of decision-making and how would it impact on the quality of the decision and the morale of your team?

Lastly imagine if, from today, every decision you made was a **group** decision. What would be the impact on the speed of decision-making and how would it impact on the quality of the decision and the morale of your team?

Think about the advantages and disadvantages of each type of decision.

Autocratic decisions are quick, but because they are made by one person may not be of a consistent high quality and it can have a negative effect on team morale if they are never consulted.

Consultation slows down the process, but quality tends to improve and the team like it if they are genuinely listened to, so morale improves. Many managers make the mistake of pretending to be consultative, while actually being autocratic.

Some group decisions are fine, but it takes longer and morale can suffer if the team feels a lack of leadership. Quality may also suffer if a majority in the team have a vested interest in a certain outcome. This style is most appropriate to mature work groups where the manager is confident the decision will be in the team's and the company's best interest, and where the length of time taken to come up with a decision is not critical to the quality of the decision. On the downside, remember those group decisions on holiday? Something like 'where are we going to eat tonight?' Deciding can take forever and someone is never satisfied. This is true of all group decisions.

Questions managers need to ask themselves are:

1. Do I have enough information to make a high quality decision now?

2. Is there more than one decision that would be acceptable?

3. Will any decision I make have a negative impact on the team and is it important that they are consulted beforehand?

4. Does the final decision matter and is there time to give it to the group to sort out?

Decision-making at work can be made easier by the fact that many problems reoccur, so your decision will most often be based on previous experience. If you manage a mature team that is well established you can delegate decision-making in the knowledge that team members have the necessary knowledge and experience to make the right decisions.

The standard model for decision-making is:

1. Define the issue

2. Collect relevant information

3. Generate feasible options

4. Work out the costs and benefits of each option

5. Make the decision

6. Implement and evaluate

Most decisions are relatively low risk and low cost. Most of the time the impact of our decision-making is negligible. For the big decisions that count we need to spend more time looking at alternatives and appraising the consequences of making a mistake. In many situations it is better to make a decision, even if it turns out to be less than perfect, than to delay decision-making while trying to find the best solution possible.

Answering the four questions above should point you towards the most appropriate style of decision to make.

QUICK RECAP

- *Don't put off difficult jobs. Tackle them early.*

- *Procrastination only causes you stress.*

- *Use lists to prioritise your time and reduce procrastination.*

- *Manage your physical files as well as your electronic files.*

- *Try to have a clear desk.*

- *Draw a map of where everything should go based on the flow of paper and information into your office.*

- *Manage the flow of paper in one of the following ways, either:*
  - *Do it now*
    OR
  - *Delegate it*
    OR
  - *File it for future action and schedule the time when you will deal with it*
    OR
  - *Get rid of it (shred, delete) unless you need to keep a paper copy*

- *Manage your incoming and outgoing telephone calls.*

- *If you are a manager use different styles of decision-making to make better use of your time and your team's time.*

CHAPTER 9

Managing time in meetings

Meetings can take up a disproportionate time at work and be great time wasters. As with presentations, meetings have a habit of simply filling up the time available without achieving very much, or in many cases over-running the time that has been allocated. This can lead to frustration among those attending the meeting and disappointment with the result.

This chapter will look at some of the basic things we get wrong when we call meetings, some tips for the chair of the meeting on how to make meetings work and how to be a better participant at meetings.

EFFECTIVE MEETINGS

Nowadays some meetings are more formal than others. In a formal meeting there will be a chairperson, a note taker (someone who takes the minutes of the meeting), a formal agenda and the minutes for the meeting will be distributed afterwards. A lot of meetings nowadays are less formal, but it is still important to follow some basic rules if you want to get the best from the time available.

Effective meetings don't happen by accident, they happen by design. Even good meetings can be better. This quote from the American comedian Milton Berle sums up many of their problems: 'A meeting is a gathering where people speak up, say nothing, and then all disagree!' There are a number of things you can do before and during a meeting to make sure it runs smoothly, on time and achieves what it is meant to.

WHY WE NEED MEETINGS

Meetings are called for a number of reasons. Generally, meetings are held:

- To inform
- To discuss
- To decide
- To sell
- To solve problems
- To advise
- To update

Meetings can be defined as 'a gathering of people sharing

common or differing objectives where communication is the primary means of achieving those objectives within the group'. An effective meeting is one where common objectives are achieved in the minimum amount of time while satisfying the needs of participants.

Most managers spend considerable amounts of time calling and attending meetings. If formal and informal meetings are taken into account this can take up well over half of the manager's day. The most common problems with meetings result from the fact that:

- The meeting has unclear objectives

- There is no clear agenda

- The meeting takes longer than necessary

- The meeting is a regular meeting that takes place regardless of need

- People attend who may not need to attend

- People making presentations over-run on time

- The chairperson does not manage the meeting well

- People arrive late

- Action points are not documented, or followed up

Meetings need not be formal affairs with attendees sitting around a table. Informal meetings in colleagues' offices can be made equally as effective if certain basic ground rules are followed. One important thing to agree at the beginning of the meeting is the overall objective of the meeting. This can be summarised in a single sentence:

'By the end of the meeting I want the group to...'

This way, by the end of the meeting, you can judge how successful it has been.

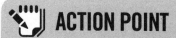

ACTION POINT

Think of a meeting you manage, or a meeting that you are about to attend. Write down the objective for the meeting. Ask someone else if they agree with your objective.

THE ROLE OF THE CHAIRPERSON

The chairperson, or chair, is responsible for managing the meeting and making sure the meeting objectives are met. Their role is to ensure that everyone is given the opportunity to take part and that no one person, or group, dominates the meeting.

There are a number of tasks the chairperson will need to complete before and during the meeting to ensure it runs smoothly. These include preparing for the meeting, managing the meeting and following up after the meeting.

Preparing for the meeting

To prepare for the meeting the chairperson should:

- Decide on the meeting's objectives

- Decide who needs to attend the meeting

- Put together an agenda and distribute it

- Arrange an appropriate venue

- Communicate with those attending about the arrangements

- Arrange for refreshments and food if appropriate

Managing the meeting

During the meeting the chairperson is responsible for :

- Making sure the meeting starts on time
- Confirming the meeting's objectives and agenda
- Confirming the 'rules' on timing, questions and participation
- Starting the meeting
- Managing the meeting by ensuring timings are kept to and that everyone has a chance to participate
- Controlling the group as appropriate
- Summarising what has been agreed as the meeting progresses
- Recording what has been agreed (unless another person has been nominated to take notes)
- Agreeing next steps and producing an action plan
- Closing the meeting

After the meeting

After the meeting has taken place the chairperson must review how the meeting went and think about ways to improve future meetings. They must make sure they follow up on the action plan.

TOP TIPS FOR RUNNING MORE EFFECTIVE MEETINGS

1. Use time wisely. Meetings have a habit of over-running, especially when you have competing egos taking part.

2. When you prepare an agenda think about:
   a. Priorities: what must be covered and how you can cover the agenda in order of importance.
   b. How will you measure the success of the meeting?
   c. Who needs to attend and, as important, who doesn't need to attend?
   d. How much time should be spent on each item?
   e. Venue, date and start/finish times

3. Think about preparation. What do people need to do to prepare for the meeting? Do you want people to make presentations, do research, or produce reports?

4. Stick to the agreed timings. If people begin to over-run at the beginning of the meeting it will force you to cut short the participation of others later on.

5. Don't allow certain individuals to get away with late timekeeping or dominating the meeting. One of the chairperson's roles is to keep discipline. Be firm, but fair.

6. Be aware of the body language of the group. Keep eye contact with team members and make sure everyone is able to participate.

7. Keep summarising what has been agreed.

8. For regular meetings, set aside some time for asking the question 'How are we doing? How could we improve the way we run our meetings?'

DEALING WITH DIFFICULT PEOPLE IN MEETINGS

In meetings problems often arise because the people who attend have conflicting objectives. One role as chairperson is to manage and resolve conflict wherever possible.

🔍 EXAMPLE

1. *I used to chair a regular meeting where there was one member of the team who regularly interrupted and gave his opinions. This became very irritating for me as chair, but also for other team members. I decided to speak to him privately rather than in the meeting itself and told him how his interrupting was causing problems for me, as chair, and for other team members.*

   He hadn't realised how irritating his behaviour was for members of the team. We agreed that if he had a point to make he would indicate to me that he wished to contribute. He also agreed to keep his interventions short and specific.

   My role was to resolve the problem without doing it too publically. The problem was resolved and the meetings ran more smoothly in the future.

2. *I also used to run a monthly meeting for my sales team. And the sales director would regularly attend. He was an important guy but was invariably late. At first we would wait for him to arrive. This caused me and the team members frustration. In the end I decided we would start on time whether or not he was there.*

   The first time we invoked the new rule, he was a bit unhappy. I took him to one side at the end of the meeting and explained the new rule and why I had implemented it. It turned out he had a lot of emails to sort out first thing in the morning, which was why he was getting delayed. Also, he didn't really need to attend the whole meeting.

   In the end we decided to give him a specific spot at the meeting, which enabled me to start the meeting on time and allowed him to get the other stuff out of the way before joining the meeting.

Here are some other examples of difficult situations you may meet:

One or more people dominating

This problem must be avoided if the chairperson is to keep control of the meeting and enable all those attending to play an active part. This typically could involve a senior member of the group or someone with specialist knowledge.

The chairperson must involve others without directly attacking the ego of the person involved. Use of assertiveness techniques (see p.135) can enable the chairperson to dissuade this type of person from dominating the meeting. For example:

'That's very interesting George. I'm sure the others will wish to add their opinions to this topic. Jane, how do you feel ...'

'Before you go on, let's get some feedback from the others...'

People not contributing

This can happen for a number of reasons:

- The person is shy and afraid or nervous of speaking

- The person is angry and refuses to speak

- The person is bored and can't be bothered to speak

Where someone is **shy or nervous** it is the chairperson's job to firstly observe who is and who is not taking part in the meeting. If the person is shy or nervous, bring them into the meeting gently, choosing subjects that you know they are confident discussing. Protect them initially from the stronger members of the group in order to build up their confidence.

Angry people may bottle up their emotions. Many chairpeople feel uncertain in these circumstances and try to avoid conflict by ignoring the situation. The problem is, the situation does not go away. It is best to get feelings out on the table while ensuring that others in the meeting are defended in the process. Keep cool, calm and logical. Ask how the person feels. Be supportive and friendly to the person even if you have to be hard on the problem.

In these circumstances the chairperson may need to stay neutral, supporting management and avoiding inter-departmental slanging matches. Where resolution of the problem is not possible focus the attention of the meeting back onto the meeting objectives and see what *can* be achieved.

If people are **bored and can't be bothered to speak** ask yourself the questions:

- Why are they bored?
- Is the meeting relevant to them?
- Should they be there?
- Is the topic under discussion relevant and important?
- Is the meeting room causing the problem?
- Do they need to be somewhere else?

Here you should assertively ask the individual what is the cause of the problem. This should be done in a non-threatening way. Explain that you are concerned that everyone gets maximum benefit from the meeting.

Conflict in meetings

Sometimes conflict in meetings is inevitable. Where a high degree of honesty and trust exists within a group of people conflict can be constructive. In many cases different personalities and competition between departments and rivalry between individuals can help solve problems and produce innovation.

This can mean:

- There is increased motivation and energy to carry out the task

- Different opinions spark off innovative solutions

- Issues are brought to the table and therefore have to be resolved

Conflict in meetings sometimes occurs because individuals fail to communicate effectively, perceive things differently, have different values and are looking for different outcomes. Part of the chairperson's role is to keep the team focused on issues rather than individuals, to sit back and listen to the perceptions of individuals, to mediate where there is genuine divergence of opinion and to remind the group of its common goals.

The chairperson should handle conflict positively by:

- Wherever possible, staying neutral

- Clarifying objectives

- Helping different sides see the other point(s) of view

- Facilitating inter-group communication

- Focusing on the problems not the individuals

- Generating alternative solutions

- Setting apparently irreconcilable differences to one side
  – (this helps save face and moves the meeting forward)

- Keeping the meeting and issues in perspective

HOW TO BE A MORE EFFECTIVE PARTICIPANT

To get the most out of attending a meeting it is important that the topics under discussion have relevance to you and your job. Here are some ideas for being a more effective participant:

Take an active part

Many chairpeople get frustrated when organising meetings because people don't proactively volunteer to participate. Can you volunteer items for the agenda? This is a great opportunity to get things discussed that you feel strongly about.

Be positive

All organisations are imperfect. It is so easy when you are working for any organisation to knock things and be negative. Try not to get a reputation for being negative. Think of the positives and promote your ideas in meetings.

Learn how to listen

I see a lot of people in meetings waiting to interrupt. If you are a fairly active member of the team with strong views and opinions it can be tempting to jump in a lot. Work on your listening skills. Try to attend a whole meeting just listening. Bet you can't do it!

Help to resolve conflict

Where there are differences, be prepared to listen to the other person's point of view. If you have a disagreement with another team member one good technique you can use is to try to describe the situation how the other person sees it. And get them to do the same. This is a very powerful problem-solving tool. Keep an open mind.

Learn presentation skills

One feature of most in-house meetings is how poor people are at presenting. Presentations over-run, the audience is not engaged and gets bored and the presenter inflicts 'death by PowerPoint'. When giving presentations make them brief and simple. People are no longer impressed by PowerPoint and all the tricks it can do.

Give feedback to the chairperson

Share your thoughts on how to improve things but also give positive praise for a job well done.

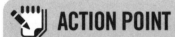 **ACTION POINT**

Here is a self-analysis checklist. It can be completed by you alone, or you can do it working with a friend or colleague. It can also be used by teams to review their own effectiveness.

1. Write down what you feel are the biggest problems that meetings cause you in your work.

2. How much of your time is spent attending meetings? (Formal and informal).

3. What proportion of your time is taken up by meetings that you consider are productive?

4. Give examples of unproductive time spent in the meetings you have attended recently.

5. How often is an agenda published prior to the meetings you attend? How effective are these agendas in practice?

6. How often is information sent out for you to read prior to attending your meetings? What effect could this have on the meetings you attend?

7. What proportion of the meetings you attend do you 'chair'?

8. What problems do you associate with chairing meetings?

9. How effective are the chairpeople at the meetings you attend? In what ways are they/are they not effective?

10. Are you confident you fully understand the 'purpose' of each meeting you attend?

11. In your opinion, how well planned are these meetings?

12. How could they have been planned better?

13. What, generally, are the outcomes of the meetings you attend? Are they generally successful, or unsuccessful?

14. How often are minutes taken and/or a record made of action agreed by those attending?

Review all of your answers to see how you can improve your meetings and make them more effective.

IMPROVING YOUR MEETINGS

Meetings are rarely perfect. However, one view of an effective meeting could be summarised as follows:

- An agenda is prepared prior to the meeting

- Meeting participants have an opportunity to contribute to the agenda in advance of the meeting

- Advance notice of meeting time and place is provided to those invited

- Meeting facilities are comfortable and adequate for the number of participants

- The meeting begins and ends on time and attendees are not made to wait for late arrivals

- The chairperson monitors how long each item takes against the agenda

- Everyone is encouraged to take part

- Where appropriate, everyone attending the meeting is given the chance to participate in decision-making

- The chairperson summarises the key points that have been discussed at the end of the meeting and agrees action plans with those who have committed themselves to carry out action as a result of the meeting

- Minutes are written up and distributed after the meeting

- Periodically, the quality of the meeting is evaluated by participants

Compare this summary to your own meetings to identify areas for improvement.

QUICK RECAP

- *Meetings can take up a disproportionate amount of your work time.*

- *There are ways you can make your meetings more effective, both as chairperson, or if you just attend meetings.*

- *Effective meetings have clear objectives. Everyone knows why they are there and what they need to achieve.*

- *An effective meeting has a clear agenda which is circulated to everyone before the meeting takes place.*

- *The chairperson has a responsibility for making things happen.*

- *One of the most important skills of an effective chairperson is to manage the time a meeting takes and the dynamics within the meeting.*

- *To be a more effective participant at meetings take an active part.*

- *Keep reviewing your meetings and keep asking the question: 'How can we do this better?'*

CHAPTER 10

Assertiveness

One of the hardest things people find to say is 'no'. Often we worry about our relationships, whether at work with our manager, or socially with a friend, or a member of our family.

Often it is easier just to agree rather than cause conflict. The problem is that if we give in too often it starts to get in the way of managing our time and can cause stress. In this chapter we will look at what we mean by being assertive and what happens to us when we aren't assertive. We will also look at some easy strategies to use that will make you more assertive.

WHAT IS ASSERTIVE BEHAVIOUR?

Assertive behaviour helps us to deal with situations, acting in our own best interest, while also respecting the interest of others. Being assertive means having the confidence to stand up for yourself, to say 'no' if you mean no and express honest opinions and feelings to others. Assertive people also allow others to win and respect other people's thoughts and feelings.

Another way to define assertiveness is to look at what it isn't. Assertiveness is not the same as aggressiveness. People who use aggressive behaviour usually have problems controlling their feelings. We have all experienced aggressive behaviour, probably both as giver and receiver. When people become aggressive it is usually because they feel threatened and they often get angry. People who are passive on the other hand tend to give in, or run away.

Either reaction, as well as causing stress, can have longer-term effects on our health. When we feel under stress, or under attack our body responds physically with what is called the 'fight or flight' response. When we feel under threat we react in the same ways our ancestors used to react generations ago when we all lived in caves. It is an in-built survival technique. For example, someone is about to attack our family and we prepare to fight. A tiger appears in the distance and we run away. What happens to us physically when we find ourselves threatened is that our heart rate increases, pumping more blood to our muscles and supplying more oxygen to our muscles, heart and lungs. Our blood receives more sugar so we can run faster, or fight harder. Our blood gets thicker so we won't bleed as much, our hearing gets better and our pupils dilate allowing us to react quicker.

🔍 EXAMPLE

I used to work with a woman called Maureen. She was a very nice person and a really hard worker. She was marketing manager for a large finance company based in Leeds. Her manager was the sales and marketing director. He was a bit of a workaholic and took on lots of projects that, strictly speaking, were outside his remit.

He would regularly set Maureen projects that were important, but nothing to do with her role and expertise. She had a real problem saying no and took on a lot of extra work. She was worried that if she didn't meet her manager's expectations she would lose her job. This was totally unfounded as she was highly respected within the company.

This is an example of how one person's bad time management practices impact on other people. She needed to work out her priorities. As marketing manager she had goals to achieve and needed to develop a more assertive attitude and learn how to say no to her manager.

I persuaded her to change the way she communicated with her manager. She had to stop just saying 'yes' and to begin negotiating. 'I am happy to take on this new project, but it will mean I will not be able to produce the marketing plan on time. Don't you think this should take priority?' Maureen needed to be assertive and say no to irrelevant tasks in order to be able to do her job properly rather than simply trying to please her manager.

Don't let people dump problems on you. Give them the problem back and let them make the choice.

TOP TIPS

WHY IS ASSERTIVE BEST?

Assertive behaviour helps us to deal with situations without feeling the need to fight, or to run away. We need to be able to be more or less assertive at different times of our lives. Imagine you have been to an expensive restaurant with your partner and receive bad service. The starters were late, the main courses were cold, the waitress was indifferent to the point of being rude and they are now trying to add a 15% service charge to the bill.

What would you do, or say in this situation?

A passive person would just put up with it, pay the bill and leave. If, as they were leaving, the manager asked if they enjoyed their meal, they would respond 'yes' and then mutter under their breath 'never coming here again'.

An aggressive person would get into an argument, shout at the waitress and refuse to pay. This may or may not achieve the desired effect, but there would at least be embarrassment all round (if not a little bloodshed).

An assertive person would stay calm and cool and would try to solve the problems early in a calm, cool way. If the problems hadn't been solved they would ask to speak with the owner, or manager, state accurately what happened and the effect it had on them as a customer, then suggest a solution. For example:

'I must say we are not very happy about the service we have received tonight. Our starters were late in arriving, the waitress was not very attentive and did not try to solve the problem, or explain the reasons for the poor service. Tonight was a special occasion so we are really disappointed with the service we received. Under the Sale of Goods Act 1979 I am entitled to pay you just 50% of the bill, without the service charge, but will agree to come back if you can sort out your service problems.'

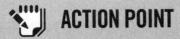

ACTION POINT

HOW TO GET STARTED

- Write down the situations where you feel you need to be more assertive

- Ask a friend, someone you trust, how assertive they think you are

- Set yourself some easy wins; situations where you can practise your assertiveness skills such as when you receive bad service, or you need to complain.

THE IMPORTANCE OF BODY LANGUAGE

When we communicate with people they interpret our message and our mood by what they see and what they hear. Albert Mehrabian, an American professor of psychology, found that the three things we are aware of when communicating with others are words, tone of voice and body language.

He said that:

- 7% of the message comes from the words we hear

- 38% from the tone of voice

- 55% from the body language we observe

While saying this may not apply to all communication, it does apply if all three are not congruent. What this means is that if we are talking to someone and ask how they are and they say 'fine', but don't look or sound fine we will believe what we see and the tone they use rather than their words.

So, body language is a crucial part of being assertive, as is the tone of voice we use and, to a lesser extent, the words we speak. Some people are naturally assertive, but it is also possible to learn assertive behaviour. Here are some tips for using assertive body language, beginning with eye contact.

Eye contact

How we make eye contact is very important. If we avoid eye contact it can make us look shifty, or nervous. If we stare at people and make too much eye contact we can be perceived as being aggressive. They say the eyes are the windows to the soul. Assertive people make eye contact but don't stare. You need to find a happy balance between focussing on the whole face and occasionally looking away as it feels more comfortable to the person you are talking to. It also makes you look more confident and assertive.

The phrase 'look me in the eye and say that' reflects that most people avoid eye contact if they are not being honest with us, or at least that's how we interpret what is going on.

TOP TIPS

It is important that you give people your full attention when communicating assertively and listen effectively. We all know how we interpret people's behaviour during a conversation when the other person keeps looking at their watch. However interested they say they are, we really know that they want to be somewhere else.

Posture

Our posture, or the way we stand and hold our body influences how people interpret our mood. Most people who feel confident angle their body towards the person they are talking to. Aggressive people stand head on and close the distance between them and the person they are communicating with.

I run presentation skills training courses and get my delegates to do short presentations that we record on DVD. People who lack confidence either put their hands behind their back, or hold them clenched together low down in front of them. My theory is that they are either trying to show they are not a threat, or defending their vital organs from attack!

Nervous people give off lots of signals that give away their mood. They wring their hands together, angle their body away from the audience and avoid eye contact, or if there is a friendly face in the audience, focus their eye contact on them. This can have a negative influence on how people perceive the presentation and the presenter.

TOP TIPS

However, you need to be careful when interpreting body language. One of the key rules is to look for more than one signal before deciding how they are feeling. Perceived wisdom says that if you cross your arms in front of your body you are being defensive, for example if you were talking to someone who had their arms crossed, with their body turned away from you with a miserable expression on their face and they said in a shaking voice 'I'm really happy', would you believe them? Of course you wouldn't. But if they had their arms crossed, but looked relaxed and happy and sounded so, we would believe them.

🔍 EXAMPLE

When I teach salespeople how to negotiate I stress the importance of changes in body language as well as congruence. So, if a salesperson presents a price and the buyer sits back, crosses their arms and looks unhappy, we conclude that the changes we observe indicate they aren't happy. Equally, if their response is to make eye contact, move closer to you, smile and rest their arms on the table, we might assume they are happy with what you have just said.

One note of caution, if you are in sales however, is that buyers are also taught about body language and have been known to fake a negative response in order to get a better discount.

Handshakes

Handshakes are also important. A good handshake should be firm, but not so hard that you pull the other person's arm out of its socket. Equally, a limp handshake indicates that they may be lacking confidence. A firm handshake accompanied with a smile sends out a more positive message.

TOP TIPS

Even if you feel nervous you can still fake confidence if you need to; actors do it all the time. How often do we hear of actors who throw up just before going on stage and go on to give a great performance? However nervous they feel, when they are on stage their body language and tone of voice convince us they are confident and competent.

Try standing up straight, taking a deep breath and looking people in the eye. You may not feel confident but you can fool others into believing you are.

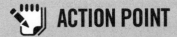 ACTION POINT

- People watch. Observe people in the street, in restaurants and at work.

- Try and assess their mood just by observing their body language.

- Think about how you present yourself through posture, body language and handshakes. Are you presenting an assertive message? What could you improve?

- Volunteer to make a speech or do a presentation at work so you can practise your posture and body language.

REACTING TO NEGATIVE BEHAVIOUR

Having successful relationships involves give and take when resolving issues. The best outcome is referred to as a win-win situation where both sides feel they have done well. We need to avoid win-lose where one side ends up feeling badly about the outcome. We certainly need to avoid lose-lose where both sides are unhappy with the outcome. However, we all experience situations when family, friends or work colleagues make us feel uncomfortable. For example:

- Your manager asks you to come to work early for a meeting then fails to arrive on time. Okay if it happens once or twice you can probably forgive it, but what if it keeps happening and they are on the phone asking you to come in early again tomorrow. What are you going to say?

- Your partner expects you to do more than your fair share of work around the house and keeps asking you to do things that he, or she has promised to do, but hasn't done. You have got into the habit of just agreeing to keep the peace, but it keeps happening. What are you going to say?

- You have a friend who keeps asking you to buy them drinks, but conveniently forgets to buy you one back, or claims, again, to have left home without any money. What are you going to say?

As you will have guessed there are three ways we might react; aggressively, passively, or assertively. If we let situations get to the point where we get angry, the danger is that we attack in a personal manner and lose our temper. This can provoke a similar reaction and an argument ensues. We use personal attacks like:

- 'You are the worst manager I have ever worked for'

- 'You are always cancelling meetings and I've had enough'

- 'You never do your fair share of work around the house'

- 'You are always breaking your promises'

- 'You never buy a drink you just sponge off other people'

- 'I'm fed up with subsidising your social life'

This kind of language doesn't help. Attacking someone personally is the wrong way to solve this type of problem. We need to tackle their behaviour, tell them how we feel, tell them how it is affecting us, but also to try and resolve the problem. We need to keep calm, but to look serious. Also, think about various outcomes that we would be happy to accept.

Here are some ideas:

- Take some time to plan what you are going to say.

- Tell them there is something you wish to talk about that is causing you a problem.

- Stick to the facts, rather than responding with an emotional outburst. Give a logical and factual account of how you see the situation.

- Tell them how you feel and how the current situation is affecting you personally.

- Suggest a solution that is fair for both of you.

- Be prepared to listen to their perception of the problem.

- Negotiate a slightly different solution if necessary as long as it is acceptable to you.

- Get their agreement to the solution and give some positive feedback once they demonstrate changes in their behaviour.

If they refuse to change, despite all your efforts you have to consider your alternatives. If you go back to where you were nothing is going to change.

TOP TIPS

- In situations like this stay objective

- Describe the situation as you see it

- Keep it objective rather than emotional

- Explore alternative solutions

- Tell your manager/partner/friend how you feel

- Look for a mutually acceptable solution

THE BENEFITS OF BEING MORE ASSERTIVE

Assertive behaviour can be learned and practised. By being more assertive you will feel more confident and less stressed. It can improve the quality of our relationships and give us more time to do the things we want to do.

Assertive people tend to be more successful at work and in their private lives. Being assertive is not just about saying no. You can't win all the time, but if you can resolve issues in a positive friendly way you will win more often.

Being able to be more assertive can reduce stress in our work and social lives. Aggressive people take up a position and defend it at all costs. Passive people tend to give in. Assertive people have the confidence and skill to resolve problems so that everybody is happy.

 ACTION POINT

Think about situations when you need to be more assertive. We all have people with whom we find it difficult to be assertive.

- Practise being assertive by saying no in low risk situations

- Make positive eye contact

- Try not to say 'I'm sorry'

- Work out what you want to ask for beforehand

- Stay calm and cool

- Tell them how you feel

- Suggest a solution but be willing to negotiate

QUICK RECAP

- *Assertive behaviour helps us to deal with situations, acting in our own best interest, while also respecting the interest of others.*

- *Stress can affect us physically and mentally. Being more assertive can help reduce stress.*

- *We are all more or less naturally assertive. It is important for all of us to decide when it is appropriate to be more or less assertive.*

- *7% of the message comes from the words we hear, 38% from the tone of voice and 55% from the body language we observe.*

- *Our body language gives away how we really feel. By working on our body language and our tone of voice we can appear to be more confident.*

- *It is important to learn how to say no and stand up for yourself without getting into a fight.*

- *Plan and practise if you are going to face a situation where you need to be more assertive and say no.*

- *Try to negotiate solutions where both sides win.*

CHAPTER 11

Communication skills

One thing that this book tries to demonstrate is that you cannot manage your time in isolation from other people. Your management of time affects you and the people around you. Being an effective communicator is an essential part of managing time. We have already seen the importance of having clear goals and how important it is to communicate these to the people around us.

In this chapter we look at the importance of good communication, the key skills involved in communication; asking questions, listening, problem-solving, presenting information, negotiating solutions and giving effective feedback.

WHY COMMUNICATION MATTERS

We have seen in various chapters of the book so far the importance of setting goals and having life and work plans. We have also seen the importance of setting priorities and being assertive. Finally then we need to be able to communicate our plans to those around us who are affected by our time management strategies and gather feedback from and give feedback to the people we are responsible for. It is also important to communicate with others so that you can take into account how their plans and time management will affect you and adjust your plans accordingly.

Effective time managers are good communicators. What does this mean? What it means is that whatever occupation you choose in life; doctor, nurse, accountant, office worker, engineer, call centre agent, housewife, nuclear scientist, you need to have good communication skills.

IMPORTANCE OF COMMUNICATING OUR PLANS

When you take the decision to produce a work or life plan it is important that you communicate this to others. Why? There are a number of reasons:

- Your plan may affect the way that others manage their time so they may need to make adjustments to their own schedule. So, for instance, if dad and mum have decided they are going to walk five miles every morning before breakfast from now on, the kids are going to have to start getting their own breakfast.

- You may want some feedback from those around you. If, as a manager you have decided to change the way you structure your meetings you are going to want some feedback from your team.

- They may want feedback from you. If your partner has decided to lose some weight a bit of positive feedback won't come amiss.

- If you have decided to delegate more responsibility to members of your team other people in your organisation will need to know.

- At the most simple level, if you are a manager you need to communicate with your team. When I got my first management job I thought everyone would just do what they were told. How wrong I was!

- Feedback is very important, but can be a bit uncomfortable. I encourage managers to work with their teams on managing the way the team works and looking for better ways of doing things. Good two way feedback is essential.

- When people work in teams within organisations they need to be constantly thinking about their personal time management, how the team manages its time and how different work teams interact. This means a constant flow of information and positive, honest feedback.

COMMUNICATION AT WORK

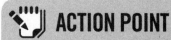 **ACTION POINT**

At your next team meeting get the team to write down five examples of when you communicate with each other. This could be by phone, by email, face to face, at meetings, or in the office.

Ask the team to rate on a scale of 1 to 10 how effective they feel these communications are and to come up with three ideas for improving each one.

Write all the ideas on a flip chart. Pick out the top 10 ideas and produce an action plan of how to implement them.

In work situations good communication is always essential. Managers need to communicate the team's goals and give instruction to make sure the goals are achieved. Standards of performance need to be set and staff need to know, on a regular basis, how they are performing and what is happening externally that will influence their day to day tasks.

When I work with clients, the biggest moan I hear is that 'no one communicates in this company'. Managers complain of a lack of communication from the people they manage and vice versa. It's always the fault of 'them up there', or 'them down there'. When I am coaching clients I like to say to them, 'when you point the finger of accusation remember, three fingers are pointing back at you!'

Effective communication can save time but it needs to be a communication method that is in itself time effective. For example if you decide to run a weekly meeting to check on the progress of an important project this has implications for the members of your team and others involved in the project. There is an 'opportunity cost' of holding the meeting because while the team is attending the meeting they are not able to do other things. As the manager, you need to decide if the 'cost' of them attending the meeting is outweighed by the benefits that attending the meeting will bring.

Without good communication we can't work efficiently and this gives us time management problems.

ASKING QUESTIONS

Asking questions is necessary for good time management and failure to ask the right questions can have a negative impact on those around us.

Q EXAMPLE

I had a client which was a large chemical company in Yorkshire. Their sales manager was a good and loyal member of staff, but not the best communicator in the world. Let's call him Mike.

He had a customer in India who rang him one day to put in an urgent order for five tonnes of a specific chemical. Mike agreed and went off to see the production manager to give him the news. The production manager was not very happy; 'we will have to run extra shifts as we don't have any of this in stock. We are very busy at the moment and it is going to be difficult to fulfil the order.'

Mike then spoke to his finance director who was equally unhappy at the financial implications; 'we will have to arrange special transport and that will add extra costs to the order.'

When Mike complained to his manager, the sales director, at their apparent lack of enthusiasm, the sales director was equally scathing; 'this order is going to cause all sorts of problems and it is unlikely we will make a profit on the deal.'

What Mike should have done was to ask more questions. What he should have asked before committing himself and the rest of the company was things like:

'How urgent is the order?'

'Do you need the whole five tonnes at once?'

'Do you realise we will need to charge a premium price for such an urgent order? Also, there will be extra transportation costs. Is that going to be okay?'

'Would you be prepared to consider an alternative product?'

What Mike failed to do, in his rush to close the deal, was receive that he needed to negotiate a mutually beneficial outcome. What he actually did was to cause all sorts of problems for colleagues in other departments. He needed to communicate better with the client on behalf of his team.

As you can see by this example asking questions is a key skill when managing your own and others' time and is vital when negotiating a mutually beneficial outcome.

There are three main types of question: open, closed and follow-up questions and each serves its purpose in different scenarios to achieve effective communication.

Open questions

These questions open up conversations and get people talking, they force the recipient to give a specific answer not simply 'yes' or 'no'. They involve key words like: 'who', 'what', 'why', 'when', 'how' and 'who'.

Here are some examples:

- 'What effect will the project have on the management team?'

- 'Why do we need a weekly meeting when we can communicate by email?'

- 'When can I expect an update on the software project?'

- 'How was your day?'

- 'Where do we need to make changes to the training programme?'

- 'Who should we invite to dinner on Friday?'

Closed questions

On the other hand, these questions seek specific pieces of information and get shorter answers, often 'yes' or 'no'. Here are some examples:

- 'Have you briefed the team?'

- 'What time does the meeting start?'

- 'Can you meet me at 9.45 on Tuesday?'

- 'Are you still coming to see me tomorrow?'

Follow-up questions

These questions can aid effective listening. The objectives of asking follow-up questions are:

- To show interest and encourage the other person to keep talking

- To increase the quality and quantity of information already gained

- To confirm understanding of information already gained

For example, by responding with 'really?' or, 'and then?' you encourage the other person to continue talking by actively showing interest in what he, or she, is saying.

Here are some examples:

- 'So, you changed your job last year. Why was that?'

- 'You say you weren't happy with your appraisal. What happened?'

- 'You mentioned changing your long-term goals. How important is that to you?'

- 'Why?'

EFFECTIVE LISTENING

Listening is a very important communication skill. Some of us are good listeners, while others find it more difficult. I work a lot with salespeople who sometimes give the impression that listening means waiting to interrupt.

Like asking questions, listening is a life skill. Barriers to effective listening include:

- The listener has pre-conceived ideas

- The listener thinks he/she knows more than the speaker

- The listener is thinking about something else

- The listener is tired or uncomfortable

- The listener is afraid of the speaker (or envious, prejudiced, or just not interested)

- The listener is anxious to input his/her own ideas

- The person speaking has a communication problem, mumbling, using jargon, has a heavy accent

- There is external noise or interruptions

Because our brains work so fast we tend to tune in and out of conversations. To listen more effectively we need to concentrate on what is being said and focus on the other person. We can use a range of verbal and non-verbal skills to become better listeners.

Verbal and non-verbal skills

Verbal skills include asking questions and summarising our understanding of what has been said. Try not to interrupt, but focus on the message. Another useful verbal listening technique is NCGs (Non-committal grunts). This is where we respond by saying 'mmm' and 'yes' and 'really' during the conversation. It's not like interrupting, but shows we are responding and encourages the other person to keep talking.

Non-verbal techniques can also help. Most of what we interpret when communicating with others comes from the body language we see. We believe this more than the words we hear. For example, you can tell when someone you are talking to wants to be somewhere else, their body language gives them away. The Albert Mehrabian 7/38/55 rule (see p.139) says that when we communicate only 7% of the message we receive comes from the words we hear, 38% comes from the tone of voice and 55% from the body language we observe.

So if someone says to us 'no, I am listening, keep talking', but their tone of voice and body language are not convincing we won't believe them.

Here are a few examples of non-verbal listening techniques you can try to become a better listener:

- Looking relaxed and at ease

- Smiling warmly

- Nodding the head

- Making regular eye contact

- Sitting still in a relaxed position

- Changing facial expression in line with what is being said

- Making notes

Listening is very important when we work in teams. If we misunderstand what we have been told it is easy to go off and do the wrong things, or misunderstand priorities. Listening is a key life and management skill.

PROBLEM-SOLVING

Problem-solving is another life skill that can make us more effective time managers. In work situations we often get problems that reoccur. The most basic fault that managers make is that they rush in to solve problems too quickly and get it wrong. Taking time to define the problem and work out the best approach can save time in the long run.

Where you have a problem to solve start by defining the problem:

- Analyse the problem. Is this something you can solve yourself or do you need to involve others in the process?

- If you do nothing will it just go away?

- Do you have the authority to solve the problem?

- Is it a recurring problem? What have we tried in the past?

Did it work?

- Generate alternative ideas. Which of these is the most cost effective and easiest solution to implement?

- Do you need to involve the team in solving the problem?

- If you come up with a solution are the team likely to support it?

Produce an action plan with specific dates and times and begin working on the problem. Make sure you review the action plan on a regular basis and make any necessary adjustments. Communicate your results to others who may experience the same problem.

PRESENTING INFORMATION

When I work with companies I see many examples of situations where misunderstanding has caused projects to go wrong, people to misunderstand their objectives and fail to identify their main priorities. If you are a manager, one of your key tasks is to brief your team and give them direction. If you work with other people it's important to be able to clearly communicate what you expect them to do.

Managing communications requires us to present information to individuals and groups. When you are presenting information or solutions to problems, the people we are communicating with are asking themselves the question 'what's in this for me?' People spend most of their time thinking about themselves and their problems, so you need to present information to them in a way that will engage their attention.

One of the first things you need to ask yourself is whether your solution is negotiable or not. Do you want the group, or individual to have an input into the solution, or is it non-negotiable? This will influence the way you present the information and determine the likely outcome.

When presenting information in this way there is a simple structure you can use. This can be summarised as:

- Tell them what you are going to tell them

- Tell them

- Tell them what you told them

When you make a presentation, be aware that your audience is asking themselves these five questions:

1. What is the purpose of this presentation?

2. What is he/she going to talk about?

3. How long will it last?

4. Can I ask questions?

5. What's in it for me?

Make sure you cover all five points when you introduce the presentation. For example when I am beginning a presentation on time management skills I begin by saying:

'Good afternoon everyone. I'm here today to talk to you about time management. My presentation will take about 45 minutes. I want to talk with you about how to identify your time management problems and to offer you a range of practical solutions to make you more effective at work.

'There will be a time at the end of the presentation for you to ask questions.

'I feel confident that by the end of the presentation you will go away with at least 20 ideas to make your management of time more efficient.'

Present your information in a logical sequence stating the background to the problem, the alternatives you have considered and your preferred solution. Finish with a summary of the key points and the next steps required. The style of presentation will be determined by the outcomes you are looking to achieve. Where the solution is non-negotiable, the presentation will be more formal. If you are looking to reach agreement the style will be more relaxed and interactive. See the section on decision-making (p.113) for more information on the most appropriate forms of decision-making.

NEGOTIATING SOLUTIONS AND REACHING AGREEMENT

Negotiation is a process of bargaining by which agreement is reached between two or more parties. As we saw in the example about Mike and the large order, we need to go through a process to reach an agreement that is acceptable to everyone involved.

🖊 ACTION POINT

You wish to change some of the working methods used by the team. Let us say for example that you want the team to be more flexible in their start and finish times because there is a really important project that needs to be completed which will involve them putting in extra work, but there is no corresponding extra financial reward to offer them.

This really is non-negotiable, but you want the team to feel motivated and gain their commitment to the project.

You may be able to offer them more flexibility with the way they manage their time, but there are limits to what you can agree to. You know you have a committed team of people who want the project to succeed, but they have some concerns about how the changes may impact on the way they work and, while you could theoretically impose a solution, it will be better if they are on your side.

How would you negotiate an agreement with your team that both you and they are happy with?

Planning a negotiation

One of the most important parts of any negotiation is the planning. I have a simple process that can be applied to any negotiation, whether it takes place at work or outside of work in social situations.

The planning process can be summarised in four parts:

1. Objectives

2. Information

3. Concessions

4. Strategy

Objectives

What is your best outcome? If you were to get everything you needed from the negotiation, what would the outcome look like? What is your worst acceptable outcome? What options are there between these two extremes? Write them down.

Information

Do you have all the information you need? Do you need to do some preparation work before the meeting? Are there questions you would want to ask during the meeting? How committed are individual team members? Do they have specific concerns you can address?

Concessions

What can you offer them other than money? What is important to them? Concessions have two elements; cost and value. The best concessions in negotiations are cheap for you to give, but valuable to them. For example you may be able to allow them to get away in good time for the weekend in return for a commitment from them to put in extra time during the week.

Strategy

You know your objectives and you know the team. What is the best way to achieve your objectives? You may need to be assertive about some issues but willing to be flexible on others.

The best way to negotiate is to put your best outcome on the table first.

TOP TIPS

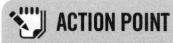

ACTION POINT

Using the earlier exercise go through the negotiation planning process and compare your answer to the one you get now. Did you reach the same agreement?

🔍 EXAMPLE

I once trained a team of people who were about to enter into an important commercial negotiation and I took them through this process. I asked the managing director, who was leading the negotiation, to ring me with some feedback after it was concluded.

'How did it go?' I asked. 'Did the preparation help?'

'No,' he said. 'It was a complete waste of time. We spent two days preparing like you told us and we put our offer on the table and they accepted it!'

He was obviously expecting a fight, but because they were well prepared they obviously looked and sounded confident and the other side felt they had a good deal.

We had a good laugh about it and he conceded that the preparation had the desired effect and maybe next time they would set their sights a bit higher.

GIVING FEEDBACK

Managers are there to manage. People need feedback if they are going to manage their time more effectively. An important part of encouraging people to change the way they do things is to give them feedback on a regular basis. When people try to change things in their lives, whether in a work, or non-work situation good feedback can encourage them to keep going while poor feedback can be de-motivating.

Giving feedback is a skill most managers need to improve. I once listened in to a manager of a telesales team giving feedback to a member of staff. She said 'that was quite good but you sounded a bit bored on the phone and interrupted the customer a few times.' This was not effective feedback as it didn't give the member of staff any idea of what they needed to improve on, just criticism of what they had done wrong.

Effective feedback needs to contain four elements. It needs to be:

1. Specific

2. Positive

3. Accurate

4. Relevant

The feedback the manager gave wasn't specific. To be specific the manager needed to give an actual example of what was said rather than a vague opinion.

The feedback was negative rather than positive. Was there something more positive she could have focused on?

The feedback was not accurate as her comments were too vague.

The feedback was relevant but by now the telesales person had tuned out of the conversation so the feedback had done no good at all.

When you give feedback you should ask questions before giving your opinion on what happened:

1. How do you think that went?

2. Talk me through the call. What happened?

3. The customer sounded a bit frustrated towards the end. Why do you think that was?

4. How could you have improved the call?

5. What are you going to do differently next time?

 ## QUICK RECAP

- *Time management doesn't just affect you, it influences and has effects on others.*

- *Good communication is important. Skills like asking questions, listening, problem-solving, presenting information, negotiating solutions and giving effective feedback affect your time management.*

- *When you produce a work or life plan you must communicate this to others who will be affected by the plan.*

- *Open, closed and follow-up questions help us to gather information and gain feedback from the people around us.*

- *Listening is an active skill we can practise that involves verbal and non-verbal communication.*

- *Problem-solving can be tackled in a structured way. Communication is an important part of the problem-solving process.*

- *When presenting information: 'Tell them what you are going to tell them. Tell them. Tell them what you told them.'*

- *Negotiating solutions is a process of bargaining by which agreement is reached between two or more parties.*

- *Feedback, to be effective, needs to be:*
  - *Specific*
  - *Positive*
  - *Accurate*
  - *Relevant*

CHAPTER 12

Your personal time management

Time management influences the whole of our lives and how we feel. Time management is not just about being more efficient at work, having a diary system that is perfect, or being able to organise our emails better than everyone else. Time management is also about you and the people around you. Time management is about how you relate to other people and manage your life as well as how you put together your filing system at work.

In this chapter we will look at managing your time outside work. We will look at the importance of managing personal relationships and why it is important to spend some of your time on you.

TIME MANAGEMENT AND YOUR LIFE

I read a quote once, which went something like 'you can find time to take out the rubbish, but you've no time to talk to your kids.' In other words, we seem to be able to achieve the urgent, unimportant stuff, mainly in our careers, but sometimes miss out on the really important things in life because they can be put off until later. Or put off forever until it's too late.

This, to me, encapsulates the essence of time management. Time management is not about achieving everything by being hyper efficient. It is about having goals, doing the important stuff that really matters and being happy.

MANAGING YOUR OWN TIME

Good time managers recognise that some things just won't get done. In most cases it doesn't matter as long as we do the important things. This relates to managing your time at work, but also managing your personal time.

We get into bad habits. Sometimes we lose sight of the important things in life and behave in ways that don't help us, or those around us.

🔍 EXAMPLE

When I set up my training business, in 1989, one of my first clients was a car parts manufacturer based in Hereford. We ran some time management classes and I remember one particular manager called John who attended the course who always looked distracted, as if he had other things on his mind.

It was a big manufacturing site and every time we had a break he would literally run out of the room and go back to his department, which was probably a quarter of a mile away from the training room. He would then come back, breathless, at the end of the break, and resume his training. Eventually I asked him what was going on. He said 'my job involves a lot of fire fighting. I need to get back on a regular basis to make sure everything is okay.'

When he dashed off at lunchtime that day one of his colleagues remarked 'there goes John. He's gone to light a few more fires so he can put them out later.'

John had a real need to feel busy and important. He saw himself as an efficient manager while in actual fact he was creating problems rather than solving them. He was a poor delegator and known within the company as a manager who was very bad at developing his staff. He was never happier than when he was dealing with a crisis, but was not seen as being an effective manager by the company that employed him. He was putting himself under immense pressure for no good reason.

What he didn't understand was that management is about achieving results through people. It's not about doing everything yourself as your team looks on.

I tried to help John, but I don't think it made much difference. What it brought home to me was the importance of being well organised, achieving objectives and working hard, through better management of your time, but not at the expense of your health and the people around you.

The problem here was that because John wasn't managing his time it had an impact on his team. He didn't trust his people to solve problems, so he tried to do it all himself. Work was everything to him. He regularly started early and worked late, yet it did not make him a successful manager. The company had concerns over his management style and were considering taking action if he didn't improve his behaviour.

The worrying thing about John was that because he regularly started work early and finished late this had an impact on his personal life. The sad thing was that despite working

long hours he wasn't seen as being particularly effective at work and his way of working had a negative impact on his life outside of work. Not only was John endangering his career through his poor time management he was making his personal life suffer through his inattention to his personal goals and the constant stress he put himself under.

Being a poor time manager meant that not only did John's work suffer but so did his personal life. Just as we have covered in previous chapters the first step to efficient time management in your personal life is to identify your goals and work out what really matters to you.

FIGURING OUT WHAT IS IMPORTANT

So, what do people say is important to them? The site www.43things.com is a useful resource that asks people about their personal goals. Looking at the top 30 goals people said they wanted to achieve, it was interesting that the vast majority didn't meet up to the SMART criteria. In chapter 2 (p.17) we discussed goal setting and its importance in good time management. SMART goals are:

- Specific

- Measurable

- Achievable

- Realistic

- Time bound

Here are 10 examples from the top 30 goals people said they wanted to achieve:

1. Lose weight

2. Write a book

3. Be happy

4. Get married

5. Travel the world

6. Learn Spanish

7. Buy a house

8. Exercise regularly

9. Take up a new hobby

10. Run a marathon

All of these goals fail the SMART test. Take the first one to lose weight. It is not specific. How much weight do you want to lose? Losing weight is certainly measurable and achievable depending on how much you decide to lose. Is the goal realistic? Yes as long as the goal isn't too ambitious. However, the goal is not time bound, because we haven't set a timescale.

A SMART objective would be something like this: I am going to lose weight. I currently weigh 170 pounds and I want to weigh 156 pounds. I want to achieve this in the next three months by dieting and taking exercise.

Once we have stated the objective the next stage is to produce a plan and put it into action.

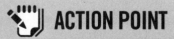 **ACTION POINT**

Take three of the goals above and rewrite them so they are SMART.

GETTING CONTROL OF YOUR PERSONAL TIME

Why are some people better organised than others? How come some people seem to achieve both a successful working life and a successful personal life?

Many of us strive to be successful at work and put a lot of time and effort into earning more money so that we can improve the living standards of ourselves and our family. The problem is that material purchases, whether it is a box of chocolates, or a new BMW, only give us short bursts of pleasure.

Good time management enables us to control many aspects of our work and personal life. Good time managers achieve the right balance between work and play and have the flexibility to respond to new opportunities.

If you are unhappy with the way you currently manage your time, a good start could be to gather some evidence. The first thing you need is data. Many people get frustrated because they feel they haven't got enough time but don't know exactly how their time is being spent. One practical thing you can do is to produce your own personal time log to find out exactly how you do spend your time and, having produced the evidence, you can begin to make changes in your life.

Writing a personal time log

We have already seen previously the importance of producing a time log of our work activities. The same can be done when we are not at work.

Frustration over the way we manage our time is often based on a vague understanding of the situation. We hear people say things like:

- 'I never have time to read books.'

- 'By the time I get back from work it is too late to do anything.'

- 'I keep meaning to go to the gym, but there are always other things I have to do.'

- 'I wish I had more time to socialise with friends.'

The purpose of a time log is to record everything you do over, say, a one week period. It is best if you can choose a typical week and not one where you are on holiday, or away on business.

We need to be able to identify our particular time management problems, at work and outside work, because until we fully understand what the problems are we cannot begin to do something about them. This is where a time log of our activity can help.

This should record all activity, in your social time, over the period showing:

- What happened

- How long it took (precise times)

- If the activity was planned

It can be a bit tedious writing everything down, especially if you have a busy life, but it is worth it. It can actually be fun. If you have a partner you can do this together. You will be surprised at the results.

What you will notice is that you spend a lot of time doing activities that fill up time, but aren't very productive. Having gathered the data try answering the following questions:

1. Looking at my social time over the period, what proportion of my time did I spend:
   a. Travelling

b. Eating

c. Socialising with friends

d. Watching television

e. On the internet

f. Reading newspapers/magazines

g. Reading books

h. Exercising

i. Talking with my partner

j. Sleeping

k. Hobbies (gardening, DIY etc)

l. Other activities (specify)

2. What am I spending too much time doing?

3. What would I like to do more?

4. What am I not doing at all?

5. How are others influencing the way I spend my time?

6. How much time could I save by planning things better?

7. What am I going to do with the time I save?

The next stage is to produce an action plan based on what you want to change. You may want to spend more time doing some things and less time doing others. Some things you might wish to stop doing altogether.

You may decide, for example, to spend less time watching television and more time eating your evening meal with your partner. You may decide to take up a new hobby like Salsa dancing, joining a choir, or joining a film club. You may decide to walk to the newsagents every morning for 15 minutes before you go to work, or you may decide to spend more time each evening in the garden.

Many people find a written plan is quite good and works for them. The main point here is to take action and to keep reviewing how you spend your social time.

TURNING AN OBJECTIVE INTO ACTION

Let us say that as a result of reading this book you decide you want to run a marathon. The distance to run a marathon is 26 miles 385 yards so you need to do a lot of training before attempting the run. To help you achieve your goal you need to complete the following steps:

1. State your objective and make it SMART. This could be: 'I will complete the London Marathon in April 2010 in a time of no more than five hours.'

2. Write down your objective and tell all your friends.

3. Write down all the things you need to do prior to the race in no particular order. For example:

   a. Get a medical check up
   b. Buy running gear
   c. Apply to enter the race
   d. Find a partner to run with
   e. Plan your diet
   f. Put together a training plan
   g. Run a half marathon by December 2009
   h. Book travel and hotel arrangements

   And so on…

4. Once you have brainstormed your list put the action points into the right order.

5. Set timescales for your action points.

6. Put the plan into action.

7. Review the plan on a regular basis and change it as required.

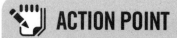

ACTION POINT

- Make a decision to take some action that will improve your family life

- Write a list of goals for you and your family

- Share your goals with others

- Put it somewhere where it can be seen

- Cross them off as they have been achieved

- If you get stuck, go back to your original plan and amend it

LOOKING AFTER YOU AND YOUR FAMILY

Your family

Nowadays the word family means different things to different people. Traditionally, the family unit consisted of a husband, a wife and children. Nowadays there are many different family groups. I would define your family as being those people you know and love and who are emotionally close to you, whether or not they live with you, or in the same town or city. What can you do to improve the way your family works together? One thing you can do is set goals for the family.

Here are some ideas:

- Sit down together and work out some common goals where the whole family can take part. Keep asking the question, 'How can we work better as a family?'

- Set aside time to eat and play together.

- Think about how the family works as a unit. Does everyone have the chance to contribute and is every member listened to and allowed to express opinions?

- Agree what is acceptable and unacceptable behaviour.

- Agree how to resolve differences that will inevitably occur.

You

Then there is you. Many people take on a lot of responsibility in their lives. They have jobs to worry about, mortgages to pay, kids to bring up, parents to look after and all the paraphernalia that comes with modern life.

One thing that time management books and courses sometimes fail to get across is the importance of looking after you. This can mean different things to different people, but my thoughts on this are that there are some key things to think about:

- Your health

- Your diet

- Your relationships

- Your spiritual side

- Things you do for you

Stick to the goals and priorities you created (see chapter 2 p.17 and chapter 4 p.45) to make sure you use time management to improve your personal life, not just your career. You meet people all the time who are so busy with work and managing their family life that they forget about themselves. Don't let yourself become one of them. Go on. Give yourself a break. Get happy!

QUICK RECAP

- *Work on managing your time outside work.*

- *Manage your social life, but also give yourself some 'you' time.*

- *Examine how you currently spend your time using a time log. Where are you now? What needs changing?*

- *Don't worry if some things don't get done as long as the important things get done.*

- *Set yourself objectives for your life, but make them SMART.*

- *Try putting together a time log for you and those around you.*

- *Decide what you want to do more of and less of.*

- *Spend more quality time with your family and friends.*

- *Look after yourself and 'don't worry be happy'!*

CHAPTER 13

Quickstart guide: summary of key points

CHAPTER 1: TIME MANAGEMENT AND YOUR LIFE

- Think about what you will do with the extra time you save from efficient time management.

- Time management can help you become better organised, however, outside influences can get in the way of your plans.

- Begin by setting yourself goals.

- Make sure that your goals relate to work, family and friends and you.

- Think about the amount of time you spend online, watching TV and reading the papers. Are there other things you would rather be doing?

- Recognise that two of the main motivators are achievement and recognition. This applies to you and the people around you.

- Motivation comes after action, not before.

- Think about the concept of 'do it now' to achieve more and clear time for the more important stuff.

- Better time management will help reduce stress.

CHAPTER 2: GOAL

- Successful time managers have clearly defined goals.

- Goals can cover all aspects of our work and non-work lives.

- Goals need to be SMART (Specific, Measurable, Achievable, Relevant, Time bound).

- Goals should be a mix of long, medium and short-term.

- Goal setting begins with an overall objective which is then broken down into a series of smaller goals.

- This leads to an action plan, which must be put into practice.

- The plan should be flexible and amended over time as things change.

- Your work-life balance is important and is about achieving a balance between achievement and enjoyment.

CHAPTER 3: GETTING STARTED

- Identify reasons why you don't change things; fear of failure, fear of success, the size of the task and the influence of others.

- Go through the four key questions to begin the process of change:
  - Where am I now?
  - Where would I like to get to?
  - How am I going to get there?
  - What's in it for me if it works?

- Motivation is about our desire and our expectations of success.

- Motivation comes after action, not before.

- Your biggest source of time management problems is you!

- Try to identify which of the five drivers you are:
  - Please people
  - Try hard
  - Be perfect
  - Be strong
  - Hurry up

- Start working on your drivers. Accentuate the positives, eliminate the negatives.

CHAPTER 4: SETTING PRIORITIES

- Make sure you manage your work and social time.

- Identify your priorities and order them accordingly.

- Begin by writing down your job purpose. This defines what your job is and where you should be concentrating your efforts.

- Categorise tasks in terms of their importance and urgency.

- Important and urgent tend to get done because they have a deadline.

- Not important and urgent tend to be done next because they also have a deadline.

- Not important and not urgent tasks tend to be done next because they tend to be easy to complete.

- Important not urgent tasks tend to get left undone unless we give them a deadline.

- Important and urgent tasks include planning, reviewing, developing, improving systems, self-development and improving relationships.

- The Pareto principle says 80% of our effective work is done in 20% of our time.

- Manage your manager. Seek guidance on your objectives and their expectations.

CHAPTER 5: PUTTING A PLAN TOGETHER

- Planning can influence the results we achieve in life and at work.

- Planning is a key part of managing your time and identifying your goals.

- Planning is an imperfect, but necessary process.

- It is important to consider short, medium and long-term goals.

- In business an important part of the planning process is to have a vision and a mission statement.

- Your business plan should include your objectives, resources, a review of the market, products and service review, an activity analysis, training plan, required resources, and your business strategy.

- Your life plan can cover all aspects of a fulfilling life, including your core values and goals for: family, finance, friends and relatives, work, health and fitness, relationships, spirituality and your relationship with society.

CHAPTER 6: USING OUTLOOK TO MANAGE YOUR TIME

- Apply the same principles of managing your emails as you do to managing your time.

- Schedule time for dealing with incoming emails.

- When you send emails make sure you don't copy everyone in. Ask yourself: is the email relevant to each recipient?

- Is it as easy to phone the person involved, or go and speak to them?

- Manage your contacts. A little effort up front saves time later.

- Group contacts as required and this gives a single email address for the group.

- Produce a To Do list daily and weekly.

- Use the calendar function to manage your meetings appointments and tasks.

- Use Outlook to produce your time plans with reminders and recurring events pre-programmed into your diary.

CHAPTER 7: DEALING WITH INTERRUPTIONS

- Understand your sources of interruptions and answer the question: 'Is it part of my job to deal with interruptions?'

- Try managing your interruptions by producing an interruptions log and analysing the results to find ways to avoid these interruptions in the future.

- Learn to delegate.

- Try to find time for uninterrupted work if this is important in helping you achieve your goals.

- Find a hiding place where you can work undisturbed.

- Decide if the next interruption can be dealt with quickly and put out of the way, or does it need scheduled time to sort it out.

- Build interruption time into your time plan.

- Learn how to say no and when to say yes.

CHAPTER 8: ESSENTIAL TIME MANAGEMENT SKILLS

- Don't put off difficult jobs. Tackle them early.

- Procrastination only causes you stress.

- Use lists to prioritise your time and reduce procrastination.

- Manage your physical files as well as your electronic files.

- Try to have a clear desk.

- Draw a map of where everything should go based on the flow of paper and information into your office.

- Manage the flow of paper in one of the following ways, either:
  - Do it now

  OR
  - Delegate it

  OR
  - File it for future action and schedule the time when you will deal with it

  OR
  - Get rid of it (shred, delete) unless you need to keep a paper copy

- Manage your incoming and outgoing telephone calls.

- If you are a manager use different styles of decision-making to make better use of your time and your team's time.

CHAPTER 9: MANAGING TIME IN MEETINGS

- Meetings can take up a disproportionate amount of your work time.

- There are ways you can make your meetings more effective, both as chairperson, or if you just attend meetings.

- Effective meetings have clear objectives. Everyone knows why they are there and what they need to achieve.

- An effective meeting has a clear agenda which is circulated to everyone before the meeting takes place.

- The chairperson has a responsibility for making things happen.

- One of the most important skills of an effective chairperson is to manage the time a meeting takes and the dynamics within the meeting.

- To be a more effective participant at meetings take an active part.

- Keep reviewing your meetings and keep asking the question: 'How can we do this better?'

CHAPTER 10: ASSERTIVENESS

- Assertive behaviour helps us to deal with situations, acting in our own best interest, while also respecting the interest of others.

- Stress can affect us physically and mentally. Being more assertive can help reduce stress.

- We are all more or less naturally assertive. It is important for all of us to decide when it is appropriate to be more or less assertive.

- 7% of the message comes from the words we hear, 38% from the tone of voice and 55% from the body language we observe.

- Our body language gives away how we really feel. By working on our body language and our tone of voice we can appear to be more confident.

- It is important to learn how to say no without getting into a fight.

- Plan and practise if you are going to face a situation where you need to be more assertive and say no.

- Try to negotiate solutions where both sides win.

CHAPTER 11: COMMUNICATION SKILLS

- Time management doesn't just affect you, it influences and has effects on others.

- Good communication is important. Skills like asking questions, listening, problem-solving, presenting information, negotiating solutions and giving effective feedback affect your time management.

- When you produce a work or life plan you must communicate this to others who will be affected by the plan.

- Open, closed and follow-up questions help us to gather information and gain feedback from the people around us.

- Listening is an active skill we can practise that involves verbal and non-verbal communication.

- Problem-solving can be tackled in a structured way. Communication is an important part of the problem-solving process.

- When presenting information: 'Tell them what you are going to tell them. Tell them. Tell them what you told them.'

- Negotiating solutions is a process of bargaining by which agreement is reached between two or more parties.

- Feedback, to be effective needs to be:

  - Specific

  - Positive

  - Accurate

  - Relevant

CHAPTER 12: YOUR PERSONAL TIME MANAGEMENT

- Work on managing your time outside work.

- Manage your social life, but also give yourself some 'you' time.

- Examine how you currently spend your time using a time log. Where are you now? What needs changing?

- Don't worry if some things don't get done as long as the important things get done.

- Set yourself objectives for your life, but make them SMART.

- Try putting together a time log for you and those around you.

- Decide what you want to do more of and less of.

- Spend more quality time with your family and friends.

- Look after yourself and 'don't worry be happy'!

CHAPTER 14

Troubleshooting

I want to get my team using their time more efficiently. Where do I start?

One good way to start is to run a brainstorming session at your team meeting. The topic should be something like 'How can we manage our time more effectively as a team?'

Here are some thoughts on running an effective brainstorming session:

1. Gather the team together and explain what is going to happen.

2. Write the topic on a flip chart and explain that you want to generate as many ideas as possible in a given timescale; say 30 minutes.

3. Explain your role, which is to facilitate the session.

4. Find a volunteer to write up the ideas on the flip chart.

5. All ideas, however wacky, should be written down and not analysed, or discarded.

6. Ideas will flow thick and fast then slow down. Encourage the team to keep thinking.

7. When the time is up start to analyse the results.

8. Agree with the group the five best ideas which are practical and are able to be implemented.

9. Produce an action plan and nominate people within the team who will champion each idea.

10. Agree a time and date to get back together and review progress.

Let the team have some ownership of managing change. Your role is to manage, not to do.

I work in an open plan office and I have a colleague who is always interrupting me. How can I do something about it without upsetting him?

This can be very annoying and difficult to deal with, especially if you are the type of person who worries about upsetting people. The problem here in psychological terms, is that you are rewarding bad behaviour and therefore encouraging it to be repeated.

Every time you stop work you and listen to this person you are saying, in effect, 'It is okay to interrupt me when you want'. So when this person is bored, or wants a chat, you are the obvious port of call. This has to change. If the interruptions mean you can't do your work it is unfair on you and this person has no right to do this to you.

Part of working with people is that there is social interaction, which is okay as long as it is kept to a sensible level.

Here are some ideas for the next time it happens. When the person comes towards you and starts talking about his social life:

1. Don't make eye contact. Continue working.

2. Tell him you are busy working on an important piece of work and don't have time to chat.

3. If you really don't want to upset him arrange a time, say lunch, when you can get together.

4. If you have got to the point where you are not worried about upsetting him and really want this to stop, make eye contact, look serious and say something like 'I can't be doing with these interruptions. You keep coming into my workspace and talking about your social life. This means I can't finish what I am working on and I would prefer it if we could leave these kind of conversations until after work. Is that okay?'

5. These people are tryers. He will be back, but if you keep

refusing to be interrupted it will stop.

This is about being assertive and understanding you have rights as well as he does.

I spend too much time at work and my family life is suffering. Any tips?

Many people have demanding jobs that involve working long hours, working shifts, or include a lot of travelling in non-work time. In our society we often measure our success, or are measured by others by the jobs we do.

What is the first thing we ask people we meet at parties? Often it is 'what do you do for a living?' So there is social pressure to be successful and work hard. The other issue is that as organisations have become leaner and fitter, the people who are left have more to do.

Another consideration is that some people just like being busy and the work fills up the available time. Sometimes we need to take stock and focus on the important things in life.

Here are some ideas:

1. Speak to your family. How do they feel about things?

2. Are you making the most of the spare time you have? Would a bit more planning improve your non-work time?

3. Do you know what you want? Think about a time in the future when this is no longer a problem. What has changed? You now have a goal to work towards.

4. One example of a goal could be that you want to take your son to football practice on a Wednesday evening. What needs to change to enable this to happen?

5. Speak to your manager. There may be alternative solutions

here. Many people now spend part of their working week working from home. Maybe you can rearrange your work schedule. Negotiate.

6. Get a new job, or train for a new skill that will enable you to change jobs. This may not be acceptable but it is an alternative.

7. Organise your work time more effectively. Achieve the important tasks and you can do less of the non-important stuff.

My manager keeps asking me to come in early for meetings then arrives late, or cancels the meeting at the last moment. What should I do?

You need to be more assertive, but you also need to have a working relationship with your manager. A few questions first:

1. How often is it happening? Is it a real problem, or a minor irritation?

2. What are his/her reasons for being late? Are they genuine?

3. What outcome are you looking for?

This issue is about being assertive, negotiating solutions and managing your manager. The worst thing you can do in a situation like this is to get angry and have an argument.

In negotiation terms this could be a lose-lose outcome. We want a win-win. However, you have rights and one of these is to be treated fairly. How would your manager have reacted if it was you that cancelled, or turned up late?

Arrange a meeting with your manager in private. Begin by stating your reason for the meeting. Keep it factual and non-emotional: 'the reason I want to talk to you is that you have asked me to come in early for a meeting four times in the last three weeks and each time you have either arrived late, or cancelled the meeting.'

'As you know I am a committed member of the team, but I would like to find a better way of doing things.'

Remember the importance of asking questions as we discussed in chapter 12 (p.153).

You need to know why the meetings were cancelled, or the manager was late. What were the meetings for and why did they have to take place early? Did your manager realise the inconvenience it was causing you? Does your manager have a solution that you would find acceptable?

People often don't realise how their own poor time management skills impact on others. It is important as a good time manager, to be assertive and to negotiate mutually beneficial outcomes.

I always seem to be doing things at the last minute. What can I do?

It may be you, or it may be someone else who is causing this problem.

As we saw in chapter 3, some of us have the personal driver we call Hurry up. Hurry up people tend to leave things until the last minute. They are good at working under time pressure and will often take on jobs with unrealistic deadlines.

What Hurry up people often fail to realise is that it is actually themselves who create these situations, either by taking on jobs with tight deadlines, or by putting work off until it has a tight deadline. The problem is, as a Hurry up person, if they get a long deadline to complete a piece of work, the buzz just isn't there.

However, another take on this question is that you may have a Hurry up manager. When you have a Hurry up manager, what happens is that they leave things to the last minute then dump them on you. What you need is data and evidence. How often is it happening? How important is the work that you are doing at the last minute? Are you prioritising your work?

With many time management issues we need to begin by analysing the situation and gathering data. Solving time management problems often means being more assertive and negotiating a better outcome, but before we act we need more evidence.

Make a time log of your activity over a five day period. Analyse the work you have done and what proportion of that work was completed at the last minute. Go back to your job purpose. What are the priorities in your job? How are you measured?

Make sure the tasks you really need to do well are scheduled into your time plan and get done to a very high standard. If you are a Hurry up person make sure you stick to your time plan. If you are asked to take on extra tasks be assertive and make sure your manager knows that your priority work will suffer if you take on extra work.

My inbox is getting out of control and I'm never on top of my emails. Where do I start?

We receive different kinds of emails so it's up to you organise them in a way which is useful and practical. Nearly 75% of the emails we receive are spam, junk mail, or viruses. So the first thing to do is to get yourself a good spam filter. Outlook has its own junk email filter, but there are a variety of other programs available that can work alongside your email program. Search Google for the various available options. These programs transfer spam to a separate folder that you can look at when you have some time and delete the stuff you don't want to keep.

Next, think about the emails you receive. Most of what you receive is called 'reference information'. In other words you don't need to take action, but the information could be useful to you at some point. Set up a series of file folders in your email system, so you can transfer these emails to the appropriate file for future reference.

The rest of your emails will require action, so we can think about how to manage these. Here are some ideas:

- Schedule time to process emails. It is naïve to think we don't want to keep looking at our emails, so be realistic. Try to limit yourself to once an hour or even just two or three times a day if you can bear it.

- You can filter your emails by date, subject or who it came from. How you manage this depends on the volume of traffic you receive.

- The preview pane in Outlook allows you to view your emails without opening them. This means you can delete stuff more quickly.

Four helpful tips when dealing with emails:

1. Delete it. Get rid of stuff you don't need.

2. Do it. Take action now and get it out of the way. Once it is done file it away somewhere other than your inbox if you need to keep a record of the email.

3. Delegate it. If it is appropriate give it to someone else then file it away, or record a future action.

4. Defer it. Leave it till later. Make a note on your calendar for future action.

Finally, if you receive a lot of emails, build time into your schedule to clean up your files and get rid of the stuff you don't need. It is no different from having a session cleaning out your filing cabinet. Find a time when you are not busy and just do it.

I am constantly interrupted by questions and problems from the team I manage. How can I reduce the number of interruptions but still be available for my team?

This is a common problem and is most likely your fault. Sorry if that sounds harsh but like the previous query on being interrupted by a colleague in an open plan office, you are allowing this to happen.

Let's get real. As a manager, part of your job is being interrupted by members of your team who need help and advice. However, if you are allowing this to happen too much, the team is not developing. Unless you have some key knowledge that no one else has, you should be encouraging the team to learn new skills and take more responsibility. In other words, **delegate**.

Begin by gathering data. Is it the whole team, or just some individuals? What are the questions and problems they are bringing you? Do they already have the skills to sort these issues out, or do they need training?

One of the problems with delegating is that it needs some up-front time to train team members how to do the task, or solve the problem.

However, if you have someone who keeps bringing you problems, but you know they have the skills, knowledge and experience to solve the problem, try this. Send them away. Tell them you are too busy to talk, and tell them to go away and sort out the problem and you will support their decision. When they have done this give them praise and encourage repeat behaviour.

Your job as a manager is to achieve results through people, not to do everyone's job yourself.

I have a very busy job, but don't seem to be getting anywhere. What should I do?

When you say you aren't getting anywhere what does this mean? You need to define exactly where it is you want to get to and begin to make plans.

You have a busy job, but you don't feel you are getting anywhere, so you need to do a number of things:

1. Review your short, medium and long-term goals.

2. Speak with your manager. How does he, or she see your current situation?

3. What opportunities do you have to move forward?

4. How well organised are you at the moment?

5. Are you prioritising your work tasks so you are doing the important stuff in your job?

6. Does your organisation run appraisals? A good appraisal interview might clarify your current situation and give you a plan of action you can begin working on.

Now that you have a clear idea of your role and goals come up with a new work plan to help you achieve those goals and fulfil your role.

I have a big project coming up and I don't know where to start. What are your thoughts?

The problem with big projects is that they can feel a bit overwhelming. You need to begin by making sure you fully understand the objective of the project. What is the outcome you are looking to achieve? If the objectives are unclear, get clarification from your manager.

Secondly, what resources do you have and what do you need? This can include people, finance and physical resources. Next you need to determine the timescales you are working to. There may need to be a negotiation here and it is better to negotiate up front than negotiating when you have a time problem.

If you have a team of people working with you put your team together and agree roles and responsibilities. Brainstorm all the steps that need to be taken to reach your objective then rewrite these in a logical sequence; assigning different steps to different people.

Once this has been done put your action plan together. Build in some extra time for the inevitable and unseen delays that will happen.

Get your plan agreed by your manager and begin working on it. It is inevitable that things will never go 100% according to plan, so the plan needs to be adjusted as you go along.

Document everything that occurs as the plan is implemented, but make sure if there is bad news you give it early and negotiate what needs to be done to put the plan back on track.

Manage the project. Get good lines of communication established between you and other team members. Avoid surprises.

As you go through the project keep everyone informed who needs to be informed and you should find that your project is a success; delivered on time and within budget.

My meetings are a disaster. They constantly over-run and we never seem to achieve anything. What am I doing wrong?

The key words here are 'disaster', 'over-run' and 'never achieve anything'.

Why are they a disaster? This is a very subjective word that is not very helpful. Define what you mean. Does it mean that you fail to achieve your objectives? Does it mean that the team feels negative about attending your meetings? Are you, as chair of the meetings, failing to perform your function properly, or does the problem lie somewhere else?

Why are the meetings running over the agreed timescale? Usually this is because the agenda is too ambitious, or that there is a lack of discipline within the meeting.

Does 'we never seem to achieve anything' reflect on the objectives you have set for the meetings?

Here are some pointers to improve your meetings:

- Before you meet define the purpose of the meeting and set your objectives.

- Write an agenda for the meeting and rank agenda items in order of importance.

- Set a time and a time limit for the meeting and stick to it. Start on time and end on time.

- Agree the rules. Set standards in relation to timekeeping and participation and clarify your role as chair.

- Decide what needs to be discussed and what can be announced. Refer back to decision-making in chapter 8. If everything becomes a group decision you are bound to over-run.

- If people are making presentations make sure they don't over-run.

- Make notes on what has been agreed for distribution afterwards. Delegate this task to different people at each meeting.

- Summarise, at the end of the meeting, what has been agreed and action points.

- Have a session periodically where your team assesses the effectiveness of your meetings.

- Give other team members a chance to chair the meeting occasionally, but brief them beforehand so they fully understand your expectations.

Index